"People from every walk of life can learn something from Ralph Heath's *Celebrating Failure*. Heath's book tells us how even the toughest failures can, in the end, fuel tremendous success. Encouraging originality, responding to changes, and thinking big are just some of the approaches Heath advocates to help people to learn from failure and achieve their dreams."

—U.S. Senator Russ Feingold

"Fear of failure is perhaps the worst affliction a manager can have because it leads to creative paralysis and inhibited growth. And the fear is understandable. Despite all the clichés coming from higher management, such as, 'We reward mistakes,' and 'If you're not making mistakes, you're not trying hard enough,' most managers know that mistakes are more often punished than rewarded. Into this cultural reality now comes Ralph Heath's reassuring words about failure not only as teacher but as a power that leads to greater success. I highly recommend this helpful book."

—James A. Autry, author of *The Servant Leader: How to Build a Creative Team, Develop Great Morale,* and *Improve Bottom-Line Performance*

"There is no better way to learn than by experience. *Celebrating Failure* shows how we can learn from our so-called failures to build a path to success. Ralph has found a fresh approach that will reduce the fear of failure and increase your confidence. I highly recommend this book for any sales professional."

—Jeff Thull, author of *Mastering the Complex Sale* and *Exceptional Selling*

"Ralph Heath shows how and why you can't go far with a small idea. He and the firm he built personify the power of taking risks and thinking big, built on the philosophy that the more mistakes you're willing to make, and the faster you learn, the better you get."

—Tim Williams, founder of Ignition Consulting Group and author of *Take a Stand for Your Brand: Building a Great Agency Brand From the Inside Out*

"Heath's account of failure and triumph is joyful and inspiring. His personal journey with failure and success is applicable to both school and business leaders. Helping students to succeed is fraught with failure, but viewing these failures as a necessary precursor to success is inspiring. If ever school leaders needed inspiration, it is today. Heath's account makes me want to share my own failures with him, experience his warm and encouraging response, and try once again to make a difference in the lives of the next generation."

—Susan H. Alexander, district administrator, Markesan District Schools, Markesan, Wisconsin

"Given the pace of change in today's business environment, developing a culture of intelligent risk-taking is no longer an option. It is merely the 'ante' to keep pace with changes in your industry, your competition, and your customers. The practical approaches outlined in *Celebrating Failure* can help you develop a healthy environment of risk-taking that is essential today and into the future."

—Gregg Billmeyer, senior director, staff operations, Office of the President and CEO, Anheuser-Busch Companies, Inc.

"Most of us focus on avoiding failure, so we take as few chances as possible. But for Ralph, failure is always a genuine option. Which is probably why he created such an interesting and successful company. Ralph's book will help every professional who most probably spends his or her life focused on avoiding failure to finally embrace it and become more successful by doing so."

—Robb High, business development consultant to the agency industry, former COO of Kirshenbaum Bond + Partners

"Forget the fear, the embarrassment, and the guilt typically associated with failure and see how it can be your greatest tool in achieving success."

—Terry Gillette, founder and former president of The Company Store

"Everyone has heard these pithy statements about embracing failure found on inspiring posters, or in graduation cards: 'Better to have tried and failed than never to have tried.' 'Nothing ventured, nothing gained.' But few know how to live those statements. In Ralph Heath's book, *Celebrating Failure*, he turns poster into practice by providing a brilliant discourse on building a corporate culture that takes you beyond those simple statements."

—Taggert J. Brooks, associate professor of economics, University of Wisconsin–La Crosse

"For the small business owner like me, Ralph Heath's message is clear: To succeed one must not strive to avoid failure but rather expect and celebrate when it appears, as it must. He provides clear thinking as to why perfection is not to be expected, and, in fact, must not be sought. *Celebrating Failure* will change your way of seeing the world."

—Joe Friel, president, TrainingBible Coaching, LLC, and TrainingPeaks, LLC

"An open and honest assessment of 30 years in management. Reading *Celebrating Failure* should quell the fears of the new hire and re-open the learning curve of the seasoned executive."

—David F. Vite, president and CEO, Illinois Retail Merchants Association

"I've come to know Ralph through our local racing cycling community, a group of people for whom failure is definitely not embraced! After reading the book, you'll understand why we appreciate his participation and the perspective he brings. He possesses the ability to look at things differently and makes you stop and think and ask, 'Why?' Enjoy the stories and his humor. We do."

—Dan Paulus, vice president, sales and marketing, Digital Technology International

"*Celebrating Failure* is a blueprint for success. Thanks for a great read!"

—Tony Stella, investment advisor, Stifel, Nicolaus & Company

"*Celebrating Failure* is a must-read for educators. Ralph Heath's examples and stories should encourage any executive or administrator to acknowledge failure as a way to grow and learn. He clearly illustrates that failure can teach you to succeed. There is so much good information for school administrators and parents, which would hopefully be passed on to kids."

—Ann Mullally, retired school principal, Lawton Chiles Elementary School, Gainesville, Florida (2003 National Distinguished Principal)

CELEBRATING
FAILURE

THE POWER OF TAKING RISKS, MAKING MISTAKES, AND THINKING BIG

RALPH HEATH

CAREER
PRESS

Franklin Lakes, N.J.

CELEBRATING FAILURE
EDITED AND TYPESET BY KARA KUMPEL
Cover design by The DesignWorks Group
Printed in the U.S.A. by Courier

To order this title, please call toll-free 1-800-CAREER-1 (NJ and Canada: 201-848-0310) to order using VISA or MasterCard, or for further information on books from Career Press.

The Career Press, Inc., 3 Tice Road, PO Box 687,
Franklin Lakes, NJ 07417
www.careerpress.com

Library of Congress Cataloging-in-Publication Data
Heath, Ralph, 1951–
    Celebrating failure : the power of taking risks, making mistakes, and
thinking big / by Ralph Heath.
        p. cm.
    Includes index.
    ISBN 978-1-60163-064-3
    1. Success in business. 2. Business failures. 3. Failure (Psychology)
    4. Risk-taking (Psychology) I. Title.

HF5386.H349 2009
650.1--dc22
                                                                    2008054043

Celebrating Failure is dedicated to my wife, Joni, who patiently listened and offered encouragement, corrected my grammar and spelling, and whose profound sense of kindness contributed to keeping a young marketing guy grounded in a business world where many have lost their way.

Acknowledgments

I want to thank all my former associates at Ovation Marketing throughout the past 30-plus years for their contributions to *Celebrating Failure*. Whether they were aware of it or not, they provided the inspiration, as this book is mostly about their efforts to thrive on the world's advertising stage from a remote location in a small town in the middle of nowhere. My associates were, and still are, a courageous group of individuals who continue to make a mark in the world of advertising or on their new career paths.

Sara Derksen, a copywriter at Ovation, encouraged me for many years to finish what I had started, and without her insights, editing, and insistence on a schedule, I fear the book might have remained one of those unaccomplished dreams, right up there with my live, "in concert" guitar performance (which remains at the top of my dreams to be completed). Perhaps some dreams are better left as aspirational, while for others the clock has run out, such as pitching in the ninth inning of the seventh game of the MLB World Series, with the bases loaded. The body has unwillingly succumbed to the aging process, but the mind never will.

Julie Hatlem, Ovation's agency creative director for 22 years and once again an associate at my new company, Heath Leadership Group, was a source of inspiration and thoughtful leadership (everything matters). I have been fortunate to surround myself with creative people such as Julie, who can zoom in on the details and then return to 30,000 feet, where I am most comfortable.

And finally, I am blessed with an incredible family. My older sisters were kind and giving to their little brother, and in so doing taught me that I could attain whatever I desire.

My mom and dad instilled in me that accomplishing those desires takes dogged determination. My greatest accomplishments, my two daughters, Ana and Natalie, provided a lot of material for this book, as kids change forever the way we look at the world.

I owe much of my leadership thinking to my mom and dad. My 90-year-old mother is a grammarian who helped proof this book and implored me to take out the "cuss" words. I toned it down. She is a feisty lady who was head of office administration for the Milwaukee Public School system in the 1980s. Many years ago, by chance at a cocktail party, a man in the room, when learning of her job position, said, "Do you realize you are taking a man's job?" The silence in the room was deafening as those who knew my mother best feared for the man's safety. Always the proper lady (she'll be horrified I placed her at a cocktail party), she refrained from physical violence and, in fact, let the comment pass. She was a feminist long before the feminist movement became popular.

My dad worked many jobs as I was growing up, but finally settled in as a financial advisor. When I was a teen we had discussions about the stock market and how it operated. I was perhaps a bit ahead of my time when I asked him about the possibility for abuse by those running the system. He assured me that our financial institutions were run by honorable people that wouldn't manipulate the system for personal gain. Sadly, he was accurately describing himself and his values that remain impeccably high. If he had been in charge, the world would be a far greater place.

Thanks for the nurturing, Mom and Dad. I love you.

Contents

Introduction: Failure Teaches You to Succeed

When you're determined to use failure as a school for success, you'll find that it's easier to hold a strategic course and refine the plan, rather than constantly second-guessing yourself. Panic subsides, along with depression, humiliation, and all the other unhappy byproducts of perceiving failure as an unmitigated disaster.
—Bill Walsh, American Football Hall of Fame coach

Failure and defeat are life's greatest teachers. One of the reasons my previous business, Ovation Marketing, thrived throughout our 31-year history was that we used our hundreds, or perhaps thousands, of failures to achieve success. Failure is the foundation upon which great companies are built. When we were at the height of youthful exuberance, we unearthed our mistakes in an experience we referred to as "the horror story of the week." Our mistakes were that frequent and horrific! And they were outstanding learning experiences.

I became concerned at one point in time that we weren't making enough mistakes (as many as we had when we were a younger company). I hoped that it was because we had learned from past mistakes and had become smarter than we once were, and not that we had stopped taking risks.

Then, as if to quell my fears, one of our people made a big mistake. She made the mistake because she attempted something innovative on her own. That is the best possible reason to make a mistake. That is what great mistakes are all about: people taking chances and making decisions to get the job done. It was an error in judgment, and as General Omar N. Bradley, five-star general and former chairman of the Joint Chiefs of Staff stated, "I learned that good judgment comes from experience and that experience grows out of mistakes."

My associate told me about her mistake at a meeting with five or six others present, and she explained quite succinctly how she had learned from it. I thought, *Great, no big deal, a mistake caused by her trying her best; now she knows what she did wrong, and she'll nail it the next time.* I then attempted to move on to a new topic, as I felt we had conquered that one. However, she continued to repeat her mistake to me two more times, as if I had been out of the room the first time she told me about it.

I asked her later, when we were alone, why she repeated the mistake two more times than she needed to. I had clearly heard her the first time and had forgiven her; actually I thought highly of her for attempting what she had, and then I dismissed the mistake in a nanosecond. She told me she had come from an environment in which mistakes were not forgiven, and she was accustomed to being reprimanded and punished for making mistakes. She was waiting for me to start reprimanding her, and, when I did not, she repeated the story again to give me another chance to give her hell. Looking back on it, it was almost comical.

The whole experience gave me reason to pause. Because each one of us has been raised differently, and because most of us have been punished in the past for making mistakes, I would never be able to proclaim to my company's diverse pool of people, "Have no fear of failure!" and expect it necessarily to be so in the next moment. (Years ago, I thought I could manage people that way; now I know better.) Today, I understand that successful business leaders and coaches must develop stories that celebrate failure and the outstanding learning experiences they provide, and then they must repeat those stories over and over again until their people understand and believe it to be so. The goal often is to counter a lifetime of learned response that failure is bad and you may be shouted at, receive a warning, or even be physically threatened, punished, or fired on the spot.

So I'll keep repeating my refrain to convince others to share my belief in the greatness of failure. My associates must work to overcome their fear of failure and mistakes because the boss believes that not only is it okay to fail, but it is a necessity. And you will not be punished.

I am absolutely convinced, after more than 30 years in business, that the quickest road to success is to possess an attitude toward failure of "no fear." To do their work well, to be successful, and to keep their companies competitive, leaders and workers on the front lines need to stick their necks out a mile every day. They have to deliver risky, edgy, breakthrough ideas, plans, presentations, advice, technology, products, leadership, bills, and more. And they have to deliver all this *fearlessly*—with no fear whatsoever of failure, rejection, or punishment.

To achieve this, leaders and managers must encourage risk and embrace failure. Doing so may be a leap of faith for many, until such time as you experience firsthand the benefits of failure. Until that time comes, I hope these stories of my spectacular failures and the lessons my associates, business, and I have learned from our failures will help inspire you to "celebrate failure."

1
Starting Fires

*Success is not the result of spontaneous
combustion. You must start yourself on fire.*
—Fred Shero, National Hockey League coach

It was a cold spring day in 1957, a Saturday as I recall. My best friend, Edgar Hoffman, and I were playing with matches, as young children sometimes do. We were in the basement of a ranch home being constructed in our Milwaukee neighborhood. Because it was a weekend, the work crew was not on the site, leaving Edgar and me free to roam about the new home construction.

Edgar and I had each constructed our own private fort within the partially built structure. Edgar had just committed the corporate sin of exaggerating his résumé by declaring he had a warm fire roaring inside his fort. I took that as a challenge. (I was freezing my butt off, and I was always the competitive one.) So that morning, in the fort, what little testosterone I did have took over, and I set out to build a bigger fire than Edgar's. Our forts were made of straw so it didn't take long for me to set off a major house fire.

Fire trucks are terrifying when you're a little boy—especially if you know you are the criminal responsible for burning down the rough construction around someone's new home. I can remember being told to go to my room and await my punishment. It was not the time to ask if I could help the firemen put out the fire. And I can remember waiting in my room, certain it would be several years before I would be allowed to see the sun again or, worse, that I would be carted away to juvenile detention.

19

I never did learn who called the fire department, but I do know it was my dad who called the police after the fire was out. He told them that his son was responsible for starting the fire. He confessed to me, years later, that it was one of the hardest things he ever had to do. I told him that I had always admired him for doing it because it was so honest, and my dad was all about honesty. (Four years later, when Dad took us to an outdoor drive-in movie theater, the ticket-taker asked the ages of everyone in the car. My dad offered up that Edgar had just turned 12 yesterday and was therefore not eligible for free admission. He bought the extra ticket for Edgar. At the time, I cringed thinking what a waste of money it was, but years later I realized that my dad was setting the example of honesty, an example that I have followed, and will follow, the rest of my life.)

> ### The Failure Factor
>
> Be honest. The brave person owns his mistakes and the lessons learned as a result.

I learned multiple extraordinary lessons the day of the fire: When you make a mistake, it is best to simply tell the truth and take your lumps. It wasn't a malicious fire; I was trying to stay warm and was merely a dumb little kid trying to compete with my best friend (who was two years older and wiser than I was).

After being sent to my room the night of the fire, I did, in fact, see the sun again. My dad knew that I was horrified by what I had done, and he didn't have to dole out extra punishment. In his wisdom, he played off of my remorse and told me he was disappointed, and knew that I could perform at a higher level the next time.

That is what presidents of companies must do. Your people are most often always trying their best to please you. Sometimes, in our frustration with an employee, we forget that most important dynamic. They already feel horrible when they make a mistake, and, most often, the best thing to do is to encourage them to reach a higher standard the next time they are given an opportunity to perform.

The great thing about making a mistake is that the bar is now moved pretty low, and you get the opportunity to rush in and correct the problem and suggest a positive solution. It is an opportunity to demonstrate that you listen, that you understand what you did wrong, and that you can solve the problem when given a second chance. Plus, everyone enjoys an underdog story of coming up from the depths of mistakes and failures to achieve success.

Ironically, I made the connection years later that starting little fires is what presidents do most often. When I started that fire at 6 years old, I was merely warming up for my ultimate job as a leader and company president.

A leader's mission is to look for opportunities to grow the business inside your company and motivate your people in that particular area of expertise to raise the bar to new heights. Even if you're running a relatively small company, similar to my former advertising agency, you can't possibly work effectively across seven or more departments to direct operations yourself. You need smart, talented, and highly motivated people who will see the little fire you lit and lead the charge to make changes inside the company to pursue even higher highs. And after you've provided the spark, small flame, or flame-throwing mechanism on each issue, you get to move on and light more fires in other departments, and thus spread the gospel of trial by fire and the lessons it teaches all of us.

The fort-building fire story is one of many sparks that led me to write this book. I'm grateful my dad set the right tone in allowing me to recover from my failure.

CHAPTER INSIGHTS
Change Your Response to Failure

- **Celebrate the lesson.** When faced with a failure by someone in your company, as a leader you must stand up and praise the individual's intention, risk-taking approach, or whatever.

Find something positive to acknowledge and celebrate. Refuse to let the negative side of failure rule you or your team. Move on quickly, applying the lesson you learned. This is critical because, if you want people to push the envelope, take risks, and go above and beyond, you must cushion the fall when a failure happens. And failures will happen.

- **Fuel the fire in your people.** The truth is, the people who fail are the very same people who succeed. They are already suffering from the disappointment of the failure and are eager to prove themselves capable. Be compassionate and give them the enthusiasm, energy, and fire to keep going. They need your full confidence and support so they can rise up and not only finish the day's work, but also come back tomorrow brimming with confidence and proposing bold new solutions.

- **Go public.** Next time you experience a failure or make a mistake of consequence, call a meeting and announce it to your team. This might scare the crap out of you before you do it, but afterward you will feel a great sense of freedom. Remember this feeling; it's the absence of fear. When you announce your mistake, also say what you learned and what you did to correct your failure (to the extent possible) or how to prevent it from happening again. Take this opportunity to show the people you lead how deep your commitment goes.

2

Resistance to Change

*There is no more delicate matter to take in hand,
nor more dangerous to conduct, nor more
doubtful of success, than to step up as a leader in
the introduction of changes. For he who inno-
vates will have for his enemies all those who are
well off under the existing order of things, and
only lukewarm supporters in those who might be
better off under the new.*
—Niccolo Machiavelli

Leaders must be protectors of new ideas. There are great
masses of people out there who love to kill new ideas
before they have a chance to take root and grow. The biggest
reason for this is that new ideas represent change, and people
seldom embrace change at the first opportunity; instead they
cling to the way they have done things in the past.

Early in my career, I served on the board of directors of a
charitable organization. The executive director of the organization had never met a new idea she liked, especially if it
came from anyone on the board, as she loathed the board of
directors. She had other leadership problems as well. Finally,
her negativity became an issue, and there was a vote held to
terminate her. It was not one of the more uplifting experiences of my life. She survived the vote but was given a very
direct and rather harsh "Plan of Improvement." She dis-
agreed with the plan, and signed it begrudgingly. One of the
biggest items on her "Plan of Improvement," which she also
loathed, was for her to embrace, or at least consider, new
ideas.

Within five minutes of the first board meeting after she had signed the Plan of Improvement, a brave member of the board raised his hand and suggested a new idea. He suggested that some new information that had just been presented to the board, which reflected positively on the organization, be woven into the standard fund-raising letter and shared with potential members who were due to renew their memberships. I thought it was an excellent idea. Yet, true to form, the executive director chopped him off at the knees, saying her accountant had told her that nobody pays any attention to that kind of positive information, and she did not want it in the fund-raising letter.

In support of the board member, I pressed the point. (I was feeling empowered by the new Plan of Improvement and tired of watching her kill every new idea brought to the meeting.) I spoke up and insisted that the idea was a good one. I was eventually given the assignment by the board to rewrite the letter and work in the new information. The executive director never was able to modify her negative management ways. Three months later, the board of directors took a second vote, and she was terminated, unanimously. It was a bold decision for a volunteer board to make.

Throughout the years, I have seen people I worked with treat new ideas the same way. An account manager would bring up an idea about improving the creative product, and a creative director would sometimes, often quite publicly, cut him or her off at the knees. Or a copywriter would come up with a new idea to improve a client's advertising, and the account manager would immediately state why the idea would not work, or he or she would use the number one idea-killer line: "We tried that before." Interestingly, there is often not a moment of hesitation from the time a new idea is expressed to the swift response of the idea killer.

Why are people so eager to cling to the past and so quick to kill new ideas? The answer is simple. Accepting a new idea requires a change in thinking. When a person has been doing something a certain way for a long time and someone else tries to enter the world they control and suggest

something counter to es-
tablished thinking, some-
thing the person perceives
as a threat, his or her first
reaction is to attack the
idea.

The Failure Factor

Overcome your fear. Don't let
the fear of change keep you
from taking risks and making
mistakes.

Is it possible to teach
people to embrace new
ideas that may be counter
to their way of thinking? There's an old yarn about ad agency
icon Bill Bernbach, one of the founders of Doyle Dane
Bernbach (DDB), who is famous for the "Think Small"
Volkswagen campaign of the 1960s. It is alleged that
Bernbach carried around a small piece of paper in his pocket
that he pulled out during heated discussions and read silently to himself. The paper said, "He may be right." When
we hear new ideas, we all need to take a deep breath, take a
step back, and say to ourselves, "He may be right."

I try to do this each time I hear a new idea, even when it
is counter to the way I think. You have to take the time to
learn how the other side thinks or you will forever be stuck
in your old ways.

The truth is that many of the ideas people offer up to
you throughout your life are outstanding ideas. The problem is only that you have never heard them before. Thus,
your instincts are to attack the idea because it runs counter
to your way of thinking. Can you imagine what would have
happened if Jonas Salk had taken his vaccine idea to a focus
group, as we do with so many great advertising campaigns
today, and said, "We are going to inject people with the polio
virus!" They would have locked him up. Instead, his idea to
fight a disease by activating the body's own natural defenses
to a weakened form of the disease was tried, saved millions
of lives, and has changed forever the way we protect ourselves from disease.

To train myself to accept new ideas, I sometimes play a
mental game. I start with the correct premise that the world
is changing rapidly and, if I do not embrace new ideas, I will

be forced to live in the past, letting the world pass me by. A business can sometimes skip small changes and still survive as a company, but if you are not on board when the big change comes, you can find yourself struggling to keep pace.

An example of this is a mistake my advertising agency made many years ago. We had invested heavily in "Compugraphic computers." (Most of you have probably never heard of them, but the cost of a single Compugraphic computer was $40,000, and it was essential to the advertising business. Compugraphics were used in the 1980s to place mechanical print on a page. You moved the cursor across the screen by entering the longitude and latitude of the location on the page, rather than pointing and clicking as we do now with the mouse.) To say that Compugraphic computers were slow and technical would be an understatement. We owned four of these dinosaurs, and they were practically brand new!

Then, lo and behold, along came a new idea: a computer from a company called Apple, and with it desktop publishing and a new, lightning-fast way to work. Our company thoroughly compared the Compugraphic computers we owned to the Apple computers we needed. The Apple blew the doors off of the old Compugraphic. Yet some people in my company, especially those who worked directly with the old Compugraphic product, clung to the outdated equipment. They were so fearful of the new product and the change they would have to undertake that they were blinded by their own analysis of the two products, which clearly showed the Apple to be far superior. Thankfully, we came to our senses, swallowed our pride, invested heavily (again) in the new Apple computer equipment, and got on board in time to be competitive in the marketplace and save my company.

CHAPTER INSIGHTS
Embrace New Ideas

- **Create an idea-friendly environment.** Make your business a place where new ideas are valuable. You can help that process by immediately giving consideration to new ideas, no matter how far out they may sound (for example, "That's certainly a unique idea, Jane. Let's give that some thought.").

- **Protect idea people.** They are often free thinkers who may occasionally drive you nuts, but are worth their weight in gold to an organization that must thrive on new ideas. New ideas are the lifeblood of an organization. Businesses, similar to people, must be adaptable. We must change or die. The choice is simple.

- **Champion new ideas.** New ideas need protectors and champions. Ideas need a shepherd to guide them through the difficult processes that are most often set up for the sole intent and purpose of killing anything new. Committees and focus groups are often the sworn enemies of new ideas. You have to do all you can to slow the attackers who are waiting to pounce and kill new ideas with phrases such as "We tried that before," "The client won't like that," "We don't have enough time," or "We don't have enough money to try that."

- **Win over the enemies of new ideas.** You are going up against formidable opponents, and you must be prepared or you will be eaten alive. You might begin by inviting them to share their ideas on how to improve an area of the business (perhaps not their own). Get them thinking of ideas and involved in the experience. You will probably hear some excellent problem-solving discussion.

Give them the responsibility of finding a way around an obstacle (that they themselves have pointed out) when they resist a new idea.

3

Think Big

*As long as you're going to be thinking
anyway, think big.*
—Donald Trump

I am involved in charitable work for an outdoor recreational area in our city building mountain-bike trails. My biggest initial challenge in working with this group was to get them to think big. Some in the group had a tendency to want to do things "on the cheap," or small scale, whereas my vision was to think big—to create one of the finest mountain-bike facilities in the Midwest.

In some ways, the experience reminds me of the early years of my former agency business. In 1982, after four years of struggling with small, local advertising accounts, I had an epiphany: We could not run a successful advertising agency from La Crosse, Wisconsin, if we continued to think small and work on local accounts. It became clear we would never grow, never be rich, if we continued to make our living doing TV commercials for local car dealers or designing logos and menus for area restaurants. We had to think big. We had to believe that we could convince the world's leading brands that we could do niche creative work for them from our remote outpost in La Crosse.

You cannot go far with a small idea, yet there is a temptation in the advertising business to propose the safe concept. Some of the reasoning behind that is based on fear: fear that the client will not approve a risky or edgy approach (and many will not), as they fear losing their jobs. However, risky and edgy creative approaches are the ones that cut through the advertising clutter and get results for the client. Sometimes big ideas cause big change—change that disturbs the safe status quo and forces a journey into the unknown. It is always a challenge to coach people to embrace change, take risks, think big, and work outside their comfort zones. But that's where big ideas live—and big ideas are the key to advertising success.

> ## The Failure Factor
>
> Get uncomfortable. Stretch yourself beyond what feels safe.

This challenge of thinking big doesn't just apply to advertising success; it's universal. People who win big, think big— and risk big. They are the people who are willing to take not just "the road less traveled," but to make a road where none existed before. Our agency worked with well-known national and global brands, yet it was oftentimes difficult for our clients to stand up and embrace edgy ideas, as they fear ridicule if the idea fails. It was easier, and safer, to keep one's head below the radar and cling to a small, safe idea. Sadly, safe ideas seldom created breakthrough sales efforts.

Wondering if your own thinking is small and safe? Ask yourself, "Where are my life choices leading me?" Are you choosing manageable change? Do you seek quick approvals? Are you taking baby steps? Are you thinking small? Do you present only safe ideas? Is your primary concern security? Are you afraid of the unknown? Afraid of failure?

Or are you envisioning the future? Excited about creating change? Seeking unconventional solutions? Inviting challenging ideas? Taking risks? Making leaps of faith? Thinking BIG?

Before you answer, consider some examples of "small thinking" about some big ideas that we take for granted today:

> *This "telephone" has too many shortcomings to be seriously considered as a means of communication. The device is inherently of no value to us.*
> —Western Union, 1876

There is no reason anyone would want a computer in their home.
—Ken Olson, president, chairman, and founder of Digital Equipment Corp., 1977

640K ought to be enough for anybody.
—Bill Gates, 1981

CHAPTER INSIGHTS
Plan as if the Future Is Already Here

- **Consider big life changes.** Set aside half an hour each week for "future planning." Ask yourself, "What's next?" Gather the most intriguing questions you can about potential changes in your business or your personal life. An example from my experience: When I thought ahead to my daughters going off to college, I thought about the types of change the event might generate in my life and how I might prepare. Among other things, it made me realize they would quickly be leaving the nest and I had better optimize my time with them now.

- **Think about bigger world changes and how they might impact your business.** Explore both positive and negative changes, such as legislative changes, economic shifts, global competition, climate change, rising energy costs, or developing new markets. How might each of these changes impact your business and your customers? How might you adapt to the changes? For example, rising energy costs will demand more efficient ways to get products or services to customers. How might your business achieve that?

- **Embrace change in your life.** Does taking risks and facing changes make you feel anxious or uncomfortable? Start with small changes: Change your morning routine. Rearrange your furniture. Try a new sport. You may be surprised how small changes such as these can put you on the path to handle bigger changes with more positive energy and enthusiasm.

  Ask yourself, "What am I afraid to change?" Change it—even if it's only in a small way to begin. Demonstrating your fearless approach to change may add energy to your own life and value to your personal and business relationships. It places you in an elite class of leaders because, while many people are busy trying to survive the moment, you are planning and creating the future.

4

Leading From the Back

To lead people, walk behind them.
—Lao Tzu

My two daughters, whom I adore, have taught me a lot about leadership. When they were young, I noticed early on that when we would go for a walk up the wooded bluffs that surround our home, if I were out front leading the walk, they would often start complaining about the difficulty of the terrain and the length of the climb. When they entered the "terrible 5s or 6s," I would have to offer encouragement and somehow placate them and try to convince them they had done this climb before and I knew they were capable of making it up the bluff through the woods. But I quickly learned that if I would hang back and let them lead out front, perhaps even pretend ever so slightly that I was under some degree of difficulty just trying to keep up with the little darlings, they would double their efforts and take on the role of the parent or leader. "Come on, Dad; this is fun; you can keep up with us." The difference in their energy output was palpable and I learned to head quickly to the back of the line whenever we went for a challenging walk. I like to think I was still leading the climb up the bluff; I was just "leading from the back," which can be a superior position to lead your children or your company. There are similarities between how we lead our children and how we lead the people we work with.

Leading from the back empowers your workforce to take responsibility and lead. If your coworkers are out front providing solutions, they are far more apt to take ownership of those ideas, and owning an idea, believing it is your own, greatly increases its chances of succeeding.

I personally found leading from the back particularly effective as I led my agency business for 30 years. It is hard to keep leadership material fresh and coworkers hanging on your every word when they've been with you for a long time. Leading from the back provided an opportunity to let my staff develop their strengths and increase their confidence.

Unfortunately, this is not the way most parents or leaders are taught to manage. Management gurus and parenting experts make you think you've got to be out front charging the hill or you are somehow weak, diminished, or not doing your job. Leading from the front is a testosterone-driven philosophy that is appropriate in some battles, but not all. For example, we once had a client who became upset because he felt that management, and me in particular, had not paid enough attention to his account. It wasn't true, as I had truly been leading from the back on this particular account, attending weekly meetings that were explicitly designed to explore ways to add executive-level strategic thinking and bring added value to our client. However, I had stood back while my associates in the company presented our ideas. (You can accomplish so much more if you don't care who receives the credit.) Perhaps I carried the strategy too far, as the client felt his company wasn't getting the attention it deserved from the top. So it is not a strategy for all times or occasions, but it can often be effective. This leadership style relates to an issue you'll find discussed often in this book: Most people want to be in control of their own destiny, and it is effective to let them lead. When I was at the front leading the kids up the bluffs, they were forced to take my path and go at my pace. They had little or no control, and

The Failure Factor

Hang back. If you want to encourage leadership in others, let them lead. Be accepting of alternative solutions that are not your own and allow failure without punishment.

that would make anyone—little people or big people—feel uncomfortable.

Some of the decisions and achievements I was most proud of at Ovation were those in which others led. For example, years ago we won a new client account that involved creating a catalog of branded merchandise for Anheuser-Busch. One of the catalogs was more than 200 pages with thousands of prices, sizes, colors, fabric content, and so on. The product information in the catalogs changed frequently and often at the last minute. The first time we did the catalog, we lost a boatload of money trying to bring the project in at the amount of time we estimated it would take us. Managing all of the SKUs (store-keeping units, or individual catalog item numbers) was killing us. The people who were most painfully aware we were failing were those on the front lines attempting to offer tremendous service to our client.

It is the job of a leader to help everyone understand the business challenge—why it is unacceptable to continue to lose money—and encourage solutions to rise up from those closest to the problem. Our team came up with a remarkable database solution we appropriately named "MasterMind" that allowed us to effectively manage all of the information. The software solution was loved equally by us and our client, Anheuser-Busch. To me, the development of MasterMind was an outstanding example of leading from the back, allowing my associates to find the right solution to the challenge.

But imagine if MasterMind had been a management solution that was simply dropped on the troops with typical march-or-die orders. I believe our chances of celebrating another failure would be remarkably high. Although MasterMind provided a helpful software solution for keeping track of a ton of information, it still required an "in the trenches" diligence to feed it all of the correct data and keep it timely. MasterMind could have been a classic case of "garbage in, garbage out," if the people using it weren't passionate about keeping it current. Who better to make certain that MasterMind succeeded than the people who created the program and had ownership in its success?

After we added MasterMind to our toolbox of services, when we would meet with potential new clients, guess which software solution our people were eager to pitch with such heartfelt sincerity that it brought a tear to your eye? Leading from the back in these situations trumps all other solutions.

It takes leaders with great self-confidence to allow others to solve the company's biggest problems. After all, most perceive that leaders are being paid the big bucks to solve the big problems. But in reality, the ultimate responsibility of the leader is to empower his or her people to find the best solutions while the leader steers the ship. If you create an environment in which future leaders can come to the front and apply their superior, firsthand, working knowledge of the situation to the problem, the company's goals will be accomplished with far greater efficiency. It will be done on the leader's watch and supported at unparalleled levels by those who created the solution.

CHAPTER INSIGHTS
Trust Your Team

- **Can you follow?** Natural leaders may often dominate a group and have difficulties playing the role of a follower. Do you feel threatened by having others lead? If you always find yourself in the leadership role, consider how you can develop more well-rounded team player abilities so you don't always have to be the leader.

- **Share control.** If you are accustomed to being in charge and calling the shots, how can you give others more control of how the work gets done? Can you break down projects and make different individuals accountable for each area? Can you let go and learn firsthand that the world will continue to spin on its axis?

- **Take a sabbatical.** If you believe you are indispensible, perhaps you are not doing a complete job of training, coaching, or grooming your staff. If you were to take a month-long vacation or sabbatical, would the organization be functional and thriving in your absence? One of a leader's responsibilities is to mentor others. Consider how you might make this more of a priority.

5

I Want to Throw Up

Victory is sweetest when you've known defeat.
— Malcolm S. Forbes

When I was in high school, I was elected captain of the swim team at a meeting several days before the season started. The vote was between the most outstanding swimmer on our team and me. The outstanding swimmer was Kurt Bruins, an incredible swimmer capable of winning the state championship in the 50-yard freestyle. The only way *I* would get to the state swim meet was if I purchased a ticket on the school activity bus. I was an extremely average swimmer in high school. However, I had just finished a season as quarterback of our football team and I have a hunch I was perceived as more of a leader than the fast swimmer, whom the coach adored and had developed as an athlete since the age of 5. Coach was literally the father that Kurt never had; Coach wasn't nearly as fond of me. In fact, because I was a football player, I think he was suspicious of my loyalties. In those days, for whatever reason, swimming and football didn't mix; I was the only football player who was also on the swim team. I enjoyed swimming and went home that night, after being voted captain, filled with pride and excitement. I told my family and friends that I had been voted captain of my swim team. That was the pinnacle of my leadership role on the swim team.

The next day at school, the coach, who wasn't at the previous night's meeting and instead had his assistant run the election, caught up to me between classes.

"Ralph, there was a problem with the vote last night. The votes don't total the number of people who were present at the meeting, and, besides, I'm shocked that Kurt wasn't voted the captain. I didn't think I even needed to go to the meeting to discuss why Kurt should be captain as I just assumed everyone would vote for him. I can't believe it was even close!"

Not exactly the ringing endorsement you want to hear from your coach the day after being elected captain of the team, but I was aware that the man was not a pillar of leadership himself. I respectfully reminded Coach that being the captain was about leadership and not necessarily about being the fastest swimmer, which I readily conceded was not a contest.

"Well, I'm troubled by this vote total," he said. "So I'm going to hold a do-over vote tonight unless you agree to be co-captain of the team with Kurt."

As I write this, with the benefit of time, it doesn't sound to me today to have been an unreasonable request. In fact, if he just would have said, "Congratulations, Ralph, and by the way, I've decided to appoint Kurt as an additional co-captain because of his unique contribution (speed) to the team," I would have welcomed Kurt as co-captain, but Coach's people and problem-solving skills were less than ideal. I was troubled by the sleaze factor he had injected into the discussion and the implication that there was something wrong with the vote, which was a red herring. He took the low road with the talk of vote counts and deals to an idealistic 17-year-old, whose role models were Muhammad Ali and John Lennon. I pretty much told him I had no interest in sharing the role under those circumstances. Besides, I didn't have anything to do with the vote outcome, as his assistant ran the meeting and tallied the votes. I told the coach I did not think a second vote was appropriate and that I could not attend the meeting anyway, because I had long-standing plans to go on a hunting trip with friends. True to my word, I did not attend. Coach did show up at the do-over vote and I was told he gave an impassioned speech to the team about why Kurt should be elected captain and, indeed, Kurt won the do-over by one vote and I was out. I had been captain of the swim team for 24 hours.

If ever someone had the right to walk into the coach's office the following Monday and quit the swim team, and own the moral high ground, it was me. And I thought briefly about it. There is something alluring about telling someone that you don't need him or his team and he can go screw himself. Quitting would have provided me a brief moment of incredible satisfaction. Instead, I chose to walk into his office and tell him that I had lost all respect for him, but I was not going to let his actions affect my swim season.

I swam that year and I enjoyed it immensely, and for an average swimmer I had a good year. I finished fifth in the 200-yard freestyle at the conference finals. My appearance in the race assured that other faster swimmers would look good.

The voting episode taught me a great lesson in life that served me well years later. The lesson I learned was not to quit. I received a lot of support from my family, friends, teachers, and other coaches at the school. Sometimes it takes a moment of personal defeat for people to step forward and tell you how much they care about you. I learned that I had friends and supporters far beyond what I had realized, and that was a good feeling and a great learning experience.

A parallel lesson occurred a short 14 years later in the dog-eat-dog business world. When you check the history of most successful advertising agencies you will find that most often in their pasts they connected successfully with a client, and both agency and client took the world by storm in one particular category. We had such an experience with our client, The Company Store, back in the 1980s and 1990s, and the relationship was not without its exciting moments.

The Company Store, one of the leading home furnishing catalogs in the country, specialized in down comforters and products for the bedroom. The company has been around in one form or another since 1911, but the current emphasis on down comforters and the bedroom started in 1983. The then president, Terry Gillette, asked me to create a direct-response ad that would sell down comforters directly from an ad in *The New York Times Magazine*, utilizing a toll-free 800 number. Before that moment, Ovation Marketing, my small Midwestern general advertising agency, had about 15 clients, and our creative work included ads for The Company Store's line of Bill Blass down outerwear, down comforters, sleeping bags, and their local factory retail outlet store. Ovation had zero experience in direct marketing at that time, but Terry and I had become personal friends and he trusted us to do a good job, even though he knew we had no experience. After our meeting, I went straight to the library to learn all I could about direct marketing, and what I learned wasn't particularly encouraging. In the early 1980s most consumers looked upon direct marketing with some disdain, as most of the goods sold were of a lower quality. This was before the era of J. Crew or Williams-Sonoma; pioneers such as Lands' End and Eddie Bauer were just starting to come into their own. Most of what I read about direct marketing said that $19.95 was an acceptable price point to sell direct, but $9.95 was even better. Terry's idea was to sell luxurious down comforters via mail order with queen-size down comforter price points ranging from $100 to $200.

We created some incredibly effective ads that told a heart-warming story about a small company in Wisconsin whose ancestors had come from Europe, where they had learned to sew fine down comforters by hand in the old European tradition. We positioned The Company Store as the same people who sold directly to the nation's largest department stores and were tired of seeing those big major retailers mark up their handmade quality products, so this was the consumer's chance to buy direct from the manufacturer, saving up to 50 percent off normal retail prices. We emphasized that they had been at the same location since 1911, and if you were unhappy for any reason they would send a UPS truck at their expense to pick up the down comforter and bring it back to La Crosse. Years later when we did the math on that free pick-up policy, we determined The Company Store was spending upwards of $300,000 sending UPS trucks to pick up returns. On volume of $100 million it seemed like a good investment that contributed greatly to their reputation of standing behind their products and making people feel comfortable putting a $130 down comforter on their credit card.

Much of this is common today, but in the time before Al Gore invented the Internet, it was pioneering. I was the copywriter and creative director, and I put my heart and soul into those initial ads and the positioning of this idealistic company. Coincidentally, my wife, Joni, was one of the first telemarketing hires Terry had made when we started running the ads with the 800 numbers. She advanced in the organization and became head of the fledgling telemarketing department. It became a real family affair. That had its unique drawbacks, as you worked for The Company Store all day and came home at night to your wife, who had also worked all day for The Company Store, and you struggled to escape from reporting on what you did at work today because you just needed a break. When Joni resigned to give birth to our first daughter, I was elated we would now have different careers. Initially it was all fun and exciting, and it felt as though we were part of a successful rocket launch.

Terry Gillette was the greatest client I ever worked for. He was entrepreneurial, as was I, and always striving to take his company to greater heights. When the company was just beginning he was obsessed with taking it to $100 million, and as soon as he passed that mark he had his eyes set on a billion. Terry and I were kindred spirits in that we were both Tom Peters service fanatics and we were both sold on continuous improvement. We were both learning about direct marketing together, and it was imperative that I continually brought Terry new ideas or he would eat me alive. I watched him eat many people alive who could not keep up with his voracious appetite for all things new and continuous improvement. He played the game at the highest level, and if you couldn't play with him you were quickly dispatched; I watched as he went through a higher-than-normal turnover. I loved working with him because I believed in what we were doing, it was fun, and continually testing new ideas was profitable for my ad agency that created all of the advertising for The Company Store.

Terry was fond of saying, "When I start a sentence, I want my agency to finish it." He credited us with being able to do that. The Company Store's direct marketing sales grew quickly, and it became clear it had the potential to outperform all of the other business units, including the division that made sleeping bags and tents for the U.S. government.

With The Company Store as our primary client, my agency had grown from 10 people to 25 people in two short years. We were hiring creative and marketing people from across the country to help support our growing business with The Company Store. We were attracting new clients, as the ad campaign we created was highly visible and other companies were inviting us to do for them what we had done for The Company Store. Business was booming. We were gearing up for the third season when, out of nowhere, Terry sat me down in his office and gave me the bad news.

Unbeknownst to me, he had been visiting agencies in New York and Chicago, as he felt his now growing business had become too big for my small La Crosse ad agency. He felt he needed a higher level of advertising help if they were going to continue to grow the business. I felt as if I had just been run over by a truck.

In the annals of agency-client business relationships this was a common occurrence. In the back of my mind I feared this day, as it was at about the same time that Datsun famously dumped the ad agency that had introduced it to the world, grew its business with unique and creative ads, and changed Datsun's name to Nissan. It happened often. A small, local agency would take the client to a certain level, the client would attract national attention, and then the small agency would get fired in favor of a well-known Madison Avenue agency. But this time it was different; now it was happening to me.

I know this is a strange analogy that not everyone will be able to relate to, but when your biggest client tells you he is entertaining the thought of other agencies I imagine that it might be like your spouse telling you he or she is sleeping with someone else. (Note: Neither of my wives ever actually indicated they were sleeping with other men, nor did I ever believe they were, but something in my creative imagination connects the pain levels of the two events.)

How could this be happening? I thought I had done everything right. I worked my heart out. I contributed my best writing work to create a highly successful advertising program. Those were *my* words in The Company Store's ads running all over the country, and they were profitable and performing at a level that was, heretofore, unheard of in direct marketing. Yet now I was being rewarded by being fired. I wanted to throw up.

Terry said I could still do some creative work for him, but he was clear that the catalog and advertising programs were all moving to one of the biggest direct-response ad agencies in Chicago. The move would be a crushing financial blow to my company, not to mention my fragile ego. He was offering a small bone as consolation, and every bone in my body wanted to tell him to go *&#$ himself.

And then, interestingly, he said, "Look, we are going down to visit the agency again on Thursday. Why don't you come along with us? We'll hide you in our group and introduce you as one of our internal marketing people so you can see firsthand how the big boys do it."

It was all I could do not to come across his desk and grab him by the neck and kill him. But I was too busy with thoughts of throwing up.

I thought back to the time when I was captain of the swim team for a day. I thought about the possible satisfaction I would receive by telling him to stick it where the sun never shines, while laying on the guilt for all the hard work and spectacular results we had achieved, and how my reward was to be fired! But I also thought about how short-lived that good feeling would be. I figured by the time I made it out to my car it would start wearing off and I would have nothing. So I once again swallowed my pride, a bigger swallow than I had ever taken, and took him up on his offer to "see how the big boys do it."

I made the trip to Chicago and they introduced me as part of their team. It was an interesting day and incredible experience. I was the proverbial Trojan Horse inside the gates of Troy taking in all the ideas I could. I remember the Chicago agency presented a direct-mail piece for a down comforter, and I read the copy and thought to myself that it was one of the most beautiful pieces of copy I had ever read. It was a long day.

> **The Failure Factor**
>
> Don't let pride control you. If you keep yourself open to every possibility and your mind positive, you will be ready if the situation turns in your favor.

Although their copy might have been more melodic than mine, when it was mailed to the house list it lost a boatload of money. That had never happened to The Company Store before, as everything we had created was profitable. The Chicago agency was also just a touch arrogant toward the small down comforter manufacturing company, which did not sit well at all with Terry, who has always thought of himself as more of a New York kind of guy than a La Crosse kind of guy. (Note: Terry now lives in Manhattan and has for the past 15 years.) I think Terry had kept me around as an insurance policy in case his new agency relationship didn't work out; or, looking back on it now with the benefit of time, I wonder if he fired me to put the fear of God in me about raising the level of my agency.

I had also made a lot of friends within The Company Store, and they were supportive of and sympathetic to my plight. They tried to help me regain what I had lost. One day, the CFO discreetly handed me an envelope and whispered, "I didn't give you this," and then walked away. When I returned to my office, I found he had provided me with the Chicago agency's rate card and what they were charging for all the work they had performed.

The arrogance, the failed advertising efforts, and the big-city charges, all combined, led to the Chicago agency's firing and our rehiring in a period of exactly 35 days. In the end, it was the best thing that ever happened to me.

Terry is the kind of leader that must check the grass on the other side of the fence. If not now, he would have done it later. The fact that it only lasted 35 days was about as good as the experience ever could have been for me. But he never strayed again, to continue with the marriage analogy, and we enjoyed a long, profitable relationship together before Terry sold the company many years later to an investment group.

Ovation worked with the investment group for several more years before they, in turn, sold the company to one of their competitors, at which time our relationship ended (more about that in Chapter 28).

After the Chicago agency was history, Terry remained fiercely loyal to Ovation. He was aware that he had a solid agency right at his doorstep. I learned my lesson and became far more aggressive at building a first-class agency in La Crosse. Terry and I continued to be close personal friends, and I traveled the world with him in search of new products for their catalogs. I became part of his management team and would routinely interview his top management hires. Ovation ran trade ads years later seeking new clients, and Terry provided the testimonial for our ad campaign using his now-famous line, "When we start a sentence, we want our agency to be able to finish it." And we could.

The Company Store, similar to most growing companies, needed a continual infusion of capital to fund its rapid growth. As its agency, we became part of the dog and pony financing road show. At one early point in the financial negotiations, Terry needed to demonstrate to Prudential, Goldman Sachs, and the recently defunct Lehman Brothers that he could raise money on his own. He asked me if I would purchase 10 percent of the company with my own money. I jumped at the chance, as I was convinced we had the right mix of talent and product to conquer America—and I was right.

I credit my old swim coach, whom I loathed, and my experience at Greenfield High School for my ability to absorb that firing, swallow my pride, and hang in there until I was able to reassert my position as the alpha marketing male at The Company Store. It is hard to quantify exactly what the financial impact of that decision was on my agency's bottom line, but I do know it was huge.

You can learn a lot as a Trojan Horse, and I would highly recommend the experience. We learned that melodic copy is not necessarily better performing sales copy. You can challenge your clients, but treat them with great respect regardless of where they are from. Charge like a big-city agency and deliver the same level of service and creative. I was also reminded that in difficult times, our family, friends, and co-workers form a valuable support group and help to cushion the fall. Tapping into that support is essential to withstand the occasional attacks on your empire. Their support is especially comforting when you feel like throwing up.

CHAPTER INSIGHTS
What Goes Down May Come Up Again

- **Whom do you have on your side?** Loyalty is pure gold. Those people who stand by us through our successes and our failures are the true source of our power and endurance. I'm grateful to my family, friends, and associates, and only hope I tell them all often enough that I love them. (They're probably tired of hearing it.)

- **Whose side are you on?** It goes both ways. The compassion or kind word you extend to someone during or after a failure can make a difference. Sometimes people need to be reminded that a failure can be a chance to start again, wiser and stronger for the experience gained. In every ending is a new beginning.

6

Pause and Celebrate the Moment

*Some people like my advice so much that they
frame it upon the wall instead of using it.*
—Gordon R. Dickson

In my more than 30 years in the ad agency business, I'm certain some of my associates wanted to shoot me, as I was occasionally perceived as never being satisfied with our efforts. I confess there was a thread of truth in their perceptions, but I feel I was misunderstood and innocent of all charges.

Allow me to illustrate the point with my own flesh and blood. My daughter told me about a public relations coup she had pulled off in her job with a nonprofit organization. She had achieved excellent coverage for one of her projects on several Minneapolis TV stations. So she called me, all excited to tell Dad about what she had accomplished. Of course I was also excited to hear her news; I congratulated her, and told her how proud I was of her. It was a beautiful moment: Daughter hits home run in Dad's playground.

And then I automatically shifted into my normal business mode, because she is essentially in my business even though she works on the client side. So there I was, thinking the way I always do: How can we take that great effort she achieved and apply our core philosophy of continuous improvement? Immediately following our beautiful father-daughter moment, I began to tell her she should go to the TV stations' Websites and get copies of the video coverage and post it to her nonprofit foundation's Website. I knew that TV stations generally leave their broadcast stories online for a short time, so I felt she needed to act quickly. I advised her to make her TV story perform double duty by e-mailing the foundation members, promoting the TV coverage, and linking it back to the video showcasing the great PR achieved for her organization, thereby enabling the foundation members who didn't see the original broadcast to view the video, while at the same time showcasing her great PR achievement. I suggested this, of course, because this is all the normal stuff I would have done for our clients.

My daughter replied that she couldn't post videos to her Website because of the lack of bandwidth on the organization's relatively modest Website, to which I, seldom paying proper attention to obstacles that are placed in my way, continued at full throttle on my continuous improvement path. Not fazed by her bandwidth challenge, I suggested she instead get the link from the TV stations, post the video on YouTube, and send an e-mail with a YouTube link in it.

She told me that posting it to YouTube was perhaps not a great option, as more conservative members might not understand why their video might appear near naked pictures of Paris Hilton. Suddenly I felt as if I was talking to an account manager about the conservative nature of one of our agency's corporate clients.

And then it happened. My daughter, whom I love and adore, said to me, "Hey, Dad, relax and enjoy the moment." Out of the mouths of babes! It was indeed time for Dad to back off and return to the celebration of her success, which I did.

I know, throughout the years, I had that same

The Failure Factor

Ask for constructive criticism. You've just scored a big win. Take a moment to celebrate, then ask a trusted friend or coworker how you might improve on the success. Be open to any comments.

chilling effect on several agency associates. Through our efforts to continuously improve, leaders can give the impression that we are not satisfied with what we just accomplished with our creative or marketing efforts. I understand how and why my actions were sometimes interpreted in such a way, but it did not accurately reflect how I felt. I was, in fact, elated! Leaders of grander efforts know they need to keep moving the effort to higher heights. I admit to enjoying shorter and more reserved celebrations than most people, followed quickly by the desire to continuously improve upon the work or effort—because everything matters.

We all celebrate success in our own unique ways. Most people are probably more similar to my daughter, who enjoys a longer celebration before taking the successful event and launching it to an ever-higher level. It's not a matter of a right way or wrong way; it is a matter of unique people working in different ways. I could perhaps moderate my enthusiasm for moving forward so quickly with more ideas, and, likewise, others need to understand I am extremely proud of what we have accomplished and my desire to improve immediately is not a negative reflection on their efforts. It is simply a desire to keep improving or to capitalize on the effort and multipurpose the creative or public relations success.

A while back, I ran across this quote in *The Wall Street Journal* from an agency creative director that offered another viewpoint: "Being a good creative is also about having an insecurity that is almost—but not quite—debilitating. The best people have trouble living in their own skin, because nothing is ever great enough."

I've never thought of myself as insecure, but perhaps that is what drives some leaders' efforts. However, I generally don't think about something not being great enough; I simply want to make it better.

In the summer of 2007, I was on a four-man cycling team that won our age division in a race. No sooner had I crossed the finish line and celebrated than I began thinking of ways to do it better next year, but those thoughts were not intended to diminish our team's outstanding effort.

I have always admired the Japanese business environment where kaizen, a dedication to continuous improvement, is the accepted cultural practice. In America, sadly, efforts to continuously improve can be interpreted as being unsatisfied with the original effort, which is not what continuous improvement is all about. Perhaps it helps explain why Japanese automakers overwhelmed the American auto industry. While Detroit celebrated at new car shows, the Japanese came up with 50 small improvements to next year's model.

As a leader in an organization or family, we owe it to those who made the effort to achieve something great to celebrate the moment in such a way that they feel good about their accomplishments. But others need to understand that the desire to continuously improve is not a negative reflection on the initial effort. It is, for example, just good business sense to take a triumphant moment and make it serve multiple purposes by promoting the triumph in ways that expose it to an ever-larger audience for an ever-longer period of time. Although I have struggled with this issue, I now understand the need for moving toward the middle by offering slower and longer celebrations. To be honest, it is a real effort for me to pause and celebrate because my head is already wrapped around the idea of trying to take the accomplishment even higher.

Elevating Continuous Improvement to a Formal Process

The television program *60 Minutes* did a piece about the Israeli Air Force and how critical its job is to the life and existence of the state of Israel. One of the things that Israeli pilots routinely do after each mission is to critique each other's flights. New pilots critique the commanders and vice versa. It floods the organization with people helping each other improve. The Air Force pilots report that the critique sessions are by far the most valuable thing they do to improve their flying skills.

I am certain that, if you have the wrong attitude, elements of the critique sessions can become quite personal and painful. Imagine being a seasoned veteran of the Israeli Air Force and having a new pilot pointing out your mistakes in front of others. The new pilot, being recently exposed to intensive basic training, may have identified some bad habits that a seasoned pilot may have acquired in time.

If you have the right attitude and embrace the critiques as a contribution to your value as a pilot, listen hard to what is being said, and visualize your error and how you can take your flying to a higher level next time, it is going to be a positive experience that you can actually look forward to as a means to improve, and, in this case, further enrich life-saving techniques. On the other hand, if you are sensitive to criticism—the pointing out of small failures—especially in front of others, you will miss an opportunity to improve your flying ability for the remainder of your time as a pilot.

There are several keys to implementing a program such as this where you work.

- First, it is important that the leader be actively engaged in this process. The leader shouldn't be the first one critiqued because it is far more important that he or she be in the audience, setting the tone for how this and future critiques will be handled.

- Second, the leader must establish that past failures are forgiven and forgotten, except as a learning tool, and comments need not be harsh or personal, but instead focus on the skills that need to be improved and how we can all do it better the next time so as to elevate everyone's performance.

- Third, the constructive comments must be clear and direct in identifying the mistake that was made and the solution proposed. The person being critiqued is already under a bit of pressure, so nuanced solutions or attempts at being clever in leading him or her to a solution should be avoided. Don't dwell on the mistake, but instead offer immensely helpful and simple solutions to lead the workers in performing even better the next time. (Take your cue from the best in the coaching profession, such as Super Bowl winner Tony Dungy, who doesn't yell and scream at his players, but instead treats them with great respect.)

It is worth remembering that a worker's most favorite thing on the job is to please the leader, so you are definitely on a much different path when you begin to point out how they can do something better. Be direct and firm, but it is not necessary to raise your voice or express disappointment or displeasure in his or her actions. You are actually elated that you are able to identify a mistake and are able to correct it so that it does not repeat itself and cost you and the organization more money in the future.

The worker's second most favorite thing on the job is to receive your public praise, so lace your critique with the hope and possibility that rectifying this error will probably make them even stronger than they already are at their craft. Be guided by the truth.

After you've established the tone of the corrective meetings, it is time for you to step up and submit yourself to the process you have guided through its start-up phase. Be patient, as I assure you, not only will your own performance be evaluated, but because you set the rules, your leadership decisions will be called into question·most often by your most junior team members—and when that happens it is magic, because you know they've had those questions in the back of their minds since they started working for you, but there was never a venue for them to ask or vent their personal opinions. Now is when you can really engage them as a mentor and explain the method to your madness. You will need to thank them profusely for pointing out the error of your ways, or for asking the tough questions, whichever the case may be. Just as you set the tone for the critiquing comments to others, you must set the tone for taking the occasional shot to the chin. And some of these people have never been in a position of leadership, so they will not always have your caring and tactful approach in their questioning. You can't let that get under your skin, as you are the consummate dispenser of wisdom and courage. If you can fine-tune this process and keep it going, it will deliver gold to your organization.

CHAPTER INSIGHTS
Pace Yourself

- **Take the pulse of your organization.** How long does the impact of a success or failure typically last? Days? Weeks? Months?
- **Acknowledge failures with positive comments.** Congratulate everyone on their efforts and remind them of the strengths and wisdom they gained from the experience. Put in perspective, a failure can do as much to motivate a team as a win.
- **Establish a policy of evaluating successes and failures.** Get everyone in the organization thinking about how to leverage success and failure to take the organization's game to the next level.

7

Frank Sinatra,
Henry Mancini, and Herb Lee

I hate careless flattery, the kind that exhausts you
in your effort to believe it.
—Wilson Mizner

When I was in college, I worked as a disc jockey (for $1.60 an hour) at an easy-listening radio station. We would run about six or seven commercials a day, play a lot of Frank Sinatra and Henry Mancini, and every 10 minutes we'd open up the microphone and say, "This is easy listening, 95.9 FM, WSPL, from La Crosse, Wisconsin." And if we were feeling really brave, we'd read 10 seconds of weather.

Herb Lee was the owner of the station. In the early 1950s, when everyone thought television would put radio out of business, Herb bought two radio stations, for peanuts. While the country was having a fire sale on radio station licenses, Herb had the vision to see that radio was always going to be around, and he made some incredible investments. I always admired that in him.

Herb Lee also gave me my first business book, *How to Win Friends and Influence People*, by Dale Carnegie. I got a lot out of the book, and it started me on a lifelong path of reading business books (and now writing one). I loved Herb Lee.

Herb was a positive man. Sometimes maybe too positive. He always had a kind and uplifting word for you. One night, my best friend, Carlos Pagan, was working the night shift at the station and he had a final exam the next day. Rather than work hard playing songs from many different artists,

> ### The Failure Factor
>
> Inspire others. Provide authentic praise when it is earned. A single word spoken with love, appreciation, or encouragement can provide the strength a person needs to persevere through challenging times.

Carlos simply put up two albums on the two turntables and proceeded to go back and forth through the album tracks. It was a much easier way to work, and Carlos was doing it so he could study for a final exam. So if you listened to the station that night it was Frank Sinatra, Henry Mancini, Frank Sinatra, Henry Mancini, and so on until he finished playing through both albums, and then he'd put up two new albums and do the same thing. It was a great way to study, but a horrible way to program a radio station, unless you were crazy about Frank Sinatra and Henry Mancini.

Herb Lee called Carlos that night. Now I don't think Herb was really listening to the show, but he loved to compliment people à la Dale Carnegie and his uplifting philosophy.

"Carlos, you're doing a great show tonight!" said Herb.

The story eventually got around to all the other announcers at the station, and everyone started playing music that same "study for a final exam" way. The station soon sounded awful, especially when an announcer had two really bad albums cued up! It was the first of many lessons I learned about complimenting your staff.

The lesson I learned was that compliments are not the kind of thing you give out too freely. If you pass out compliments too easily, simply for the sake of inspiring those who work for you, it may have unintended negative consequences: It can lower the quality of work because people will say to themselves, "Hey, that was easy. I didn't even do my best work, but if that's what the boss likes, I'll give him more of the same."

So now when I tell people they've done a nice job, which is often, I make certain they have, indeed, done a nice job.

People know when you are sincere, and appreciate it that much more. If you compliment people when it is truly deserved, the kind words have their intended effect and the employees of the radio station, the advertising agency, or any type of business perform at a much higher level.

CHAPTER INSIGHTS
Be Sincere

- **Walk around.** In-person contacts carry more value now than ever because of our society's busy pace and emphasis on the efficiency of phone calls, text messages, and e-mails. Make time to deliver your compliment in person when you can. Walk to their office; don't summon them to yours. Chances are, you'll make someone's day.

- **Write a card or letter.** Too old-fashioned? That's what makes it special: people don't often take the time to do it anymore. It's a thoughtful way to thank people, congratulate them, commend their performance, or even reward them with a token of your appreciation tucked inside.

- **Acknowledge the team.** Sometimes you've got a whole office full of people who contributed to a successful project or winning a new account. One of Ovation's rituals was to ring a bell and gather as a group in the front lobby to welcome a new account onboard. It was a simple thing that cost nothing but a few moments of people's time to share the good news. Find ways to celebrate outstanding accomplishments with simple things like bagels and fruit smoothies, or team-building events like golf outings and group boating trips.

- **Success and failure.** If this book leaves you with one thought, I'd like it to be that successes *and* failures should both be lauded. Acknowledging a failure is a different type of celebration, to be sure, but failures also take our best efforts, most creative ideas, and long, hard hours of work. We most always come away from failures better for the experience. And that is worth celebrating!

8

Hire for Attitude

Nothing in the world can take the place of persistence. Talent will not; nothing is more common than unsuccessful men with talent. Genius will not; unrewarded genius is almost a proverb. Education will not; the world is full of educated derelicts. Persistence and determination alone are omnipotent.

—Calvin Coolidge

Throughout the course of my career, I've been guided by the following: "Hire for attitude; train for skill." Hiring is not exclusively about finding people with the right experience; it's about finding people with the right mindset. What people know is less important than what they are made of. It has certainly proven true with hires at our company.

Attitude being equal, when my business would hire new associates, we attempted to hire experienced people. We positioned all of our employment advertising to attract the attention of those with the most experience. But when there are not experienced people available, we're not afraid to hire inexperienced people and train them. That's why the right attitude is so important: it can make up for a lack of experience.

I know from my experience running an advertising agency in a small city in the Midwest that it is challenging to uproot experienced people from good jobs in big cities and entice them to move to a small town. Not impossible; just difficult. If an experienced advertising professional worked for a Chicago agency and wanted to change agencies, for whatever reason, he or she could choose from dozens of outstanding agencies. In La Crosse, that was not the case. Thus, people who lived in larger cities were more cautious about accepting a job here. We got very good at finding these people and making them comfortable with moving to La Crosse, but it was a continual challenge.

We were also fortunate to have trailing spouses of executives from other area companies arrive at our doorstep unexpectedly, happily possessing agency experience. We often hired these people, even when we did not have a current need. Many years ago when I was wild, crazy, and inexperienced, my receptionist buzzed me and said there was a woman at the front desk who had worked at Ogilvy Advertising in New York and wondered if I could meet with her. She was in town house-hunting for the day, as her husband had just been hired as a professor at the University of Wisconsin–La Crosse. I seldom take walk-in appointments, but something about her story sounded plausible so I went out front to speak with her. Next I invited her into my office, read her impressive résumé, and spoke with her for maybe an hour. She had a wealth of experience and the right attitude, and, although we weren't specifically in need of a copywriter, it was rare that someone of her caliber and experience would just show up at my doorstep. I offered her a job right on the spot, without checking her references, or consulting with our human resources director or our agency creative director. I've grown a lot in the job. I would never do such a thing now. I must admit it is still painful to tell this story, but the title of this book is *Celebrating Failure*, and this was one more of my learning experiences. First, you need to have human resources and the department manager on board before making hiring decisions. People want (and deserve) to be in control of their own departments. My eagerness that day took away their control and forced an exciting employee on them when, had I had more patience, that would not have been necessary. In my inexperienced brain's defense, I thought, *Hey, this is a no-brainer. You'd have to be crazy not to hire this person.* She was that good. And although that was true, I know now it is best to go through the process.

Second, my eagerness scared our new hire, as she confessed to me years later after a long and wonderful relationship (that ended only when her husband moved on to another job opportunity). Live by the sword, die by the sword. I have learned throughout the years to control my enthusiasm when a winner walks into my office, and she was a winner; I just needed to refrain from drooling in her presence. We seek most what we cannot have, so at least try to play a little hard to get. Or pretend you want to think about it overnight before making a job offer.

Third and finally, check those references carefully. When I managed a radio station earlier in my career, I hired a new announcer who had recently moved to town. I hired him at around 10 in the morning, and later that afternoon he was arrested for shoplifting steaks in a local grocery store. He listed me as his employer when he got busted. I had to sheepishly explain the embarrassment to the station owners. Not one of my best leadership days.

Needless to say, the agency refined its hiring process and developed an exemplary track record. We were able to boast of a lower-than-industry-average turnover rate of 6.3 percent for 20 years. (Keeping turnover low is money in the bank for any company.) By comparison, the last time turnover rate was measured in the advertising industry it was more than 30 percent. In 2007, when we inquired about the advertising industry employee turnover rate, we were told it was no longer measured because, as the American Association of Advertising Agencies' (AAAA) representative put it, "Our members do not want us to collect such data as it may lead to bad public relations for the industry."

> **The Failure Factor**
>
> Maintain a positive attitude. Learning from failure experiences provides growth opportunities. Keep a positive attitude and believe that you will create a new outcome with the next challenge.

CHAPTER INSIGHTS
Keep Turnover Low

My philosophy has always been to keep turnover low and retain a company's best performers. Here are strategies to achieve those goals:

- Provide opportunities for associates to grow and learn.
- Maintain associate ownership in the company.
- Create a warm, caring, and nurturing work environment.
- Empower associates to take responsibility for their own work.
- Involve associates in the direction of the company's growth and management. Invite their input formally and informally as to how the company should be run, and implement those suggestions whenever possible.
- Expect top performance. Celebrate failures. Coach and train for continual improvement.
- Let associates know when they perform well and when they need to perform better. Schedule regular reviews and let people know how they are performing.
- Attempt to reduce the stress level by promoting a healthy lifestyle.
- Seek out customers and clients who share the same belief system. Resign accounts or "fire" customers if they fail to treat us with the respect and dignity that we give them. We deliver the finest products and service, but do not take abuse.
- Be an open-book company. Share company financial information (except specific individual salaries).
- Share the vision of the company. Let your staff know where it is going and how it is going to get there.

- Treat associates with respect and compassion when personal tragedies impinge on work responsibilities.
- Pay associates the best salary possible based on the financial performance of the company. Reward them for outstanding job performance.
- Take great care in hiring, always taking attitude and character into account.

9

Family, God, and the Green Bay Packers

The greatest accomplishment is not in never falling, but in rising again after you fall.
—Vince Lombardi

Vince Lombardi was one of my childhood heroes. I grew up in Milwaukee, Wisconsin, during the Packers' dynasty years. I read his book, *Run to Daylight*, and watched as he coached at the old Milwaukee County Stadium, probably the worst venue in the world to watch a football game, because the park was built for baseball, but no one cared because we loved the Packers and Lombardi.

Vince Lombardi was legendary for his tough policies and strict management style. Jerry Kramer, who threw the infamous block that sprung Bart Starr into the end zone on the frozen tundra during the Ice Bowl, the 1967 NFL Championship game between the Packers and the Dallas Cowboys, said, rather harshly of Lombardi, "He treats us all the same—like dogs." Lombardi was most definitely a tough management kind of guy.

But Vince Lombardi had his business priorities straight. He stated them as family, God, and the Green Bay Packers. He put them in that order of importance for a specific reason. Lombardi wisely knew that family had no rival, and placed it ahead of everything else—including his beloved Green Bay Packers. That may be a hard lesson today for over-zealous management types.

> ## The Failure Factor
>
> Put people first. Family, friends, coworkers, people on the street, and you. As we're out there risking, failing, and succeeding, if we put human needs first, profit has a way of following.

It is inevitable at a place of business that the people who work for you will be confronted with personal tragedy in their lives: the death of a family member, illness, divorce, or other personal tragedy. When such a tragedy occurred to any of my associates, I met with them in person, or called them, and told them how sorry I was to hear of their problem and asked if there was anything I could do. (Note: Out of necessity, sometimes this conversation must be done through voice mail or e-mail, as the individual was oftentimes consumed by the tragedy and not available to talk face to face.) I then told them that I understood this was a very personal time for them and we wanted them to know we had all of their work covered, and they should focus all of their energy and attention on their family and not give a thought to work. They should take their time and not feel rushed to come back to work until they had done all they needed to do for their family. I explained that on a scale of one to 10, family is a 10 and work is insignificant at this moment in their lives.

In effect, I gave them a blank check to take whatever time they needed to get through their family crisis. I can't think of one time when there was even a hint of anyone abusing this offer. In fact, it was just the opposite, and I was amazed at how soon they returned to work. I understood that there was a reason for that as well. I was careful to explain that, if they wanted to come back to work and be surrounded by their "work family," we would understand that as well. Sometimes the best therapy is to keep busy, and it can be a relief to lose yourself in the work you love. I have escaped grief through work myself. The last thing you want is people passing judgment that you should be home alone grieving rather than at work surrounded by your friends.

For some people, work is a better choice; for others it clearly is not. Most importantly, the decision is the associate's to make and we whole-heartedly supported whatever decision they would make during their time of crisis. Invariably, each time after the event played out, I was thanked profusely by my associate and told how much they appreciated our position. When you expect your associates to go the extra mile for your company in tough situations, the company must be able to respond in kind when associates are faced with a crisis. The people who worked at Ovation knew that sometimes they would need to dig down deep and give up a weekend or evening to meet a critical client deadlines. It wasn't something I needed to tell them in a memo. They just knew when it was time and they simply did it. They also knew that we wouldn't abuse them, but emergencies happened from time to time and they understood. When you demanded that kind of work ethic from your people, you had to reciprocate when they were in a tough personal situation. Our approach to tragedy probably did more to promote loyalty within the organization than any other single thing we did. And it was so basic and simple, and so much the right thing to do, it is hard to believe the world doesn't universally embrace this philosophy.

Several years ago, an associate came and thanked me for the kindness we had demonstrated regarding a tragedy in her family with her mother. She had resolved the family crisis as best she could and was now returning to work, and she was thanking me for being so understanding and caring during her time of grief. She then volunteered that her sister had had quite a different experience at her place of employment. When the sister said she needed to take time off for the same crisis, her boss said, and I am quoting, "I know you'll make the right decision for the company." Good grief! No pun intended, but what a ridiculously dumb thing to say to an employee already in agony over personal tragedy in her family and probably worried sick about her job to begin with, as inevitably your best, brightest, and most conscientious employees will tend to needlessly worry the most about the caliber of the work. It's like someone has put a knife in their back and the boss has seen fit to twist it. That manager should have been summarily executed and the event should have been broadcast in high broadband on the Internet for the world to see. It is that type of management that gave birth to unions.

Tragedy affords us the opportunity to learn what we are made of as leaders and demonstrate it clearly to our employees. Tragedy is the time for those in power to hear the leadership bell and storm to the front and lead. It is a time for leaders to earn their pay and to demonstrate the company's value system and show what kind of leaders they are under difficult circumstances. Take the highest road you can imagine—then make certain you don't miss the opportunity to take it even higher. Vince Lombardi, a tough guy in a tough sport, knew that family trumped even my beloved world-champion Green Bay Packers.

CHAPTER INSIGHTS
Don't Fail to Get Your Priorities Straight

- **What's on your to-do list?** Chances are if it's like most people's, it's filled with "important" work projects and errands. If you think about the most important people in your life, what is on your list today to do with or for them?

- **Who's on your mind?** We're all busy communicating constantly these days with phone calls, text messages, e-mails, and instant messages. But are we taking the time to really connect? Forget about all the "urgent" day-to-day stuff. Take 15 minutes and sit down with a coworker and get to know him or her better.

- **Make a memory.** Family traditions, fun activities, and special events stay with us for a lifetime. Sometimes it only takes a little planning to pull off the spontaneous gift of an afternoon adventure to a ball game, park, or community volunteer activity with a child or friend. A well-rounded leader is a stronger leader.

10

Learn From Your Mistakes

*If you don't make mistakes, you're not working
on hard enough problems. And that's a big
mistake.*

—F. Wilezek

I had an interesting conversation with one of my associates that I would like to share. He said, "Ralph, why are you so quick to point out your mistakes to the entire company?"

An excellent question. Pointing out my own mistakes has indeed been a planned part of my management philosophy. I do it because I cannot keep repeating that it is perfectly acceptable for the people around me to make mistakes in their work, and yet pretend that I never make them. What better way to send a message to the entire organization that it is okay to make mistakes than to point out my own?

I should clarify that I am talking about bold mistakes, mistakes that come from taking risks, not about failing to do your job professionally. (Sending a letter with typos to a client because you did not use spell-check or skipped proof-reading is not a mistake. It is unprofessional.)

I encourage people with whom I work to take risks, and publicly attempt to reward risk-takers, especially when they fail. It is essential to be free of the fear of making mistakes. Yet, it is difficult to drive fear out of an organization.

Why do we hesitate to go back in time and attempt to learn from our own failures? The short answer is, because it can be painful. It takes a certain level of understanding and self-confidence to examine your own mistakes. Unfortunately, self-confidence is not present in all people. Leaders must create an environment where the workers understand it is not only okay, but essential to make mistakes on their way to greatness. When you believe positively that mistakes are a key part of the process and path to success, it takes away the burden of making the mistake.

Each of us has no doubt experienced, at one time or another in our lives, a "whack on the side of the head" whenever we made a mistake.

One vivid example I remember from first grade is "Here's your test. You have three wrong answers!" It nearly broke my young spirit to see that written on the top of the paper I worked so hard to complete and presented with great pride and enthusiasm to the teacher, whom I adored and admired. And what did I get for my effort? A big red mark with a check that said *minus three*. In reality, I had 97 percent of the answers right, a remarkable achievement that should have triggered spontaneous jubilation and great celebration. But that is not the way our educational system grows and instills self-confidence in our future business leaders. Instead, we beat them up and tell them, in red, that they screwed up and had three wrong. It starts there and just gets worse. Educators have helped make many people petrified of errors, but the responsibility is also shared with a host of others—most of them well-meaning parents, spouses, friends, religious authorities, coworkers, and employers. Yet for a company to be successful, its people cannot be afraid to make errors. They must actually make hundreds of mistakes *fearlessly* as part of the process of learning what works and how to succeed.

I thought my response to my associate, in which I proudly pointed out my own mistakes, was a good one, and I was filled with confidence about the truth of what I had said.

The associate then said, "Yes, Ralph, but in our society we don't tolerate mistakes from our leaders." I gave that a lot of thought. Sadly, I fear my associate had spoken the truth. You can see it in presidential elections. Each time one of the candidates makes a mistake, the numbers in the polls plummet. Elections are won or lost by the candidate who plays it safe and does not rock the boat, because a mistake can mark a candidate as a loser. Worse, the cover-up of a mistake can mark him as a criminal.

Consider this: I heard a politician talking about controlled burns in New Mexico that were set intentionally by wildlife management workers to clear the underbrush. Unfortunately, one of the fires got out of control and caused great damage to thousands of acres. The politician said, "We'll find out who made the mistake and remove that person from their position." This demonstrates the opposite of my philosophy. I believe there is no one better to do the next planned burn project than the guy who screwed up the last one, learned exactly what he did wrong, and how he should do it better the next time. After all, this person just burned a sizable acreage of New Mexico and has certainly learned from that mistake. Surely that decision-maker would be a better gamble than an inexperienced new person.

Mistakes are learning experiences that propel you toward success. Because of their learning experiences, these people deserve more money as they become more valuable to the enterprise. There is no better way to reward and reinforce risk-taking and bold deeds than by rewarding mistakes and failures.

> **The Failure Factor**
>
> Make more mistakes. If you're not making mistakes, you're going for the sure win, working below your potential, and avoiding risks.

And although it's possible to learn from others' mistakes, the lessons we learn from our own misjudgments are the most indelibly etched on our psyche—for better or worse. Sometimes a leader can be most supportive when he or she lets an associate try and fail with a risky idea, than by citing previous wisdom and dictating a course of action. It's a tough call.

In any case, I believe we need to learn to accept mistakes in leaders as well as in coworkers. Acceptance cannot be only for the mistakes of our coworkers and peer group. There must be absolute forgiveness for everyone, including managers and company presidents.

Leaders, by virtue of their position on the firing line, have the potential to make more mistakes. Their mistakes are often highly visible, with many witnesses, and they often involve large amounts of money. Because leaders have power, they are sometimes able to conceal their mistakes. That would be wrong, as you could lose the benefit of learning from the mistakes. Send the message to the organization that it's okay to make mistakes when attempting bold, new initiatives, initiatives that are the lifeblood and future of your organization.

You cannot buy or plan the kind of education that mistakes and failure provide. They demonstrate that you are out there on the front lines, taking risks, and giving your best effort. Learning from your mistakes and failures makes you more valuable to any company. People who are confident in their abilities are not afraid to share their blunders. Rejoice in your mistakes and failures, celebrate as you gain experience "the hard way," and learn the valuable lessons that mistakes and failure have to teach you.

CHAPTER INSIGHTS
Turn Failure Into a Lesson About Success

- **Have the "balls" to fail.** Years ago, the ad agency I led lost an agency shootout. (A shootout is agency slang for the competitive pitches that are presented to win a new client.) Five agencies had been invited to stand up in front of six strangers and tell them how they would better target and redesign the Kotex Website, which the client felt needed improvement. (I'm not making this up!) The site we had been asked to redesign was confusing to the consumer. It had too many different selling ideas on the home page and no single idea stood out on the site. To demonstrate the confusion the consumer feels while on the Website, our creative director proposed dumping multiple-colored balls on the conference room table to simulate the confusing choices that consumers were presented with on the home page. I jumped out of my chair, as I am, after all, the head cheerleader. Someone responded to my direction to be theatrical during business development presentations, and so I threw my support behind the dramatic, attention-getting, "balls on the conference table" idea. We arrived at the presentation, and, at the appropriate moment, our creative director reached under the table and let loose 50 multi-colored balls on the conference room table. (I'm thinking to myself, *We should have brought even more balls.*) It was pretty dramatic and we felt good about the balls on the way home.

Weeks later, we learned that we were not the chosen agency. Usually the prospective client tells you that you came in second to make you feel better. We've been second in almost every pitch we've ever lost. But we weren't even second in this one! When we did an in-depth, post-presentation interview with the people who invited us to do the pitch, we learned that they hated the balls on the conference table. One of the brand managers actually said they felt "threatened" by the balls. Who would have guessed? Although it failed to win the account, I still believe it was an excellent illustration of the confusion the consumer faced and I applaud the creative director's idea.

- **Reject fear.** Imagine that you're the leader at the company that presented the "balls on the table" idea. You know you've won many new business presentations in the past, and you remind yourself that the dramatic approach helped you win many of those presentations. You

further remind yourself you operated a successful ad agency for 30 years, without the aid of a
prestigious Madison Avenue address, so you
must continue to be bold and decisive with dramatic presentations. Yet, because of this single
failure, fear of taking creative risks begins to
permeate your organization. You hear it raise
its ugly head at the next shootout rehearsal when
your creative director has a dramatic idea that
might help put you over the top. She presents
it, and one of the professional idea killers within
your organization says, "Remember, we tried that
dramatic thing at Kotex, and they felt threatened by it. Let's play it safe and hope we stand
out anyway." Wrong. Playing it safe is a sure path
to mediocrity. If you want to succeed, to win,
you must take risks.

- **Reward risk-takers.** How do you kill the fear
of failure when it is growing within your organization? As leader you must take action. At the
following week's company meeting, you stand
up in front of everyone and present substantial
cash reward to the creative director who had the
balls to suggest the balls. You celebrate the failure in the most visible way possible and publicly
reward and praise her. The bold idea approach
didn't work that particular time, but we know
bold ideas have worked before and will work
again. We want to keep pushing bold and dramatic ideas. Thus the "legend of the balls" turns
from failure to celebration, and the troops will
work overtime to come up with the next big,
bold (ballsy) idea.

11

Pushing Yourself to Fail

*Unless you're pushing yourself, you're not living
to the fullest. You can't be afraid to fail, but
unless you fail, you haven't pushed hard enough.
If you look at successful people and happy
people, they fail a lot, because they're constantly
trying to go further and expand.*

—Dean Karnazes

Dean Karnazes is an ultramarathoner who made the statement I've quoted above in an interview that appeared in the January 2007 issue of *Outside* magazine.* Dean understands how to apply the lessons from the drama of athletic competition to his broader life and the world around him, as his quote accurately describes the attitude of a sound business philosophy. Companies and employees with the highest performance have the lowest fear of failure—and a high failure rate. Surprised? They have a high failure rate because they are comfortable with failure as a vehicle for growth. Rather than be embarrassed by failure, they wear it as a badge of honor. They are always experimenting, trying to find the next great idea that will take them or their clients out of their comfort zones, to reach new highs of business success. Sadly, most people, and particularly conservative corporate cultures, don't want to go there. Instead they choose to play it safe, to fly below the radar, repeating the same safe choices over and over again. They operate under the belief that, if they make no waves, they attract no attention; no one will yell at them for failing because they generally never attempt anything great at which they could possibly fail (or succeed).

Most corporate environments don't support risk-taking, and failure is neither encouraged nor (gasp!) rewarded.

I observed how this lack of risk-taking played a role in Ovation's potential clients' organizations. We routinely became involved in agency shootouts in which we were invited by large corporations to compete against other agencies for the corporation's advertising and marketing business. We would win about one third of these shootouts. We would lose about one third, and in about one third of the shootouts no work is ever awarded. If we could identify the one third of those potential clients who are so conflicted they aren't going to award any work, and the one third for which there is little or no synergy (and thus they probably wouldn't hire us anyway), we could have saved a lot of time and money.

Fully 80 percent of the ad dollars spent in the United States are controlled by four large advertising holding companies. We noticed when we were pitching certain conservative corporate clients we could identify as strongly risk-averse, and we were competing against one of the "holding company" ad agencies for the business, we could oftentimes tie a shootout loss back to the risk-averse nature of the company. In other words, it takes a certain amount of guts in a conservative environment to hire Ovation Marketing from La Crosse, Wisconsin, when it is considerably safer to hire JWT (J. Walter Thompson) from Chicago, Illinois.

If you choose JWT, you don't need to explain your decision. People who are knowledgeable about the advertising industry understand JWT to be a well-established brand, owned by one of the four large advertising holding companies, staffed with people who create excellent work. Those facts make it a safe choice.

However, if you *did* choose Ovation Marketing, you had some explaining to do. Everyone instantly understood why you would pick one of the best-known agencies, but a small independent agency in La Crosse that oftentimes marches to a slightly different beat? Why would you choose it? It actually wasn't difficult to explain, and we most often cheerfully helped them with the positioning as part of the presentation. It took a special kind of client to embrace us, a client who was more accepting of risk, more entrepreneurial in spirit, and who worked in the type of corporate culture in which they could stand up, take a risk, and "do some explaining" without having their legs chopped out from under them. This quality is probably one of the contributing reasons why clients stayed an average of seven years with us, versus three years for agencies that belong to the four holding companies (as reported by the American Association of Advertising Agencies, a trade group to which we belonged).

Throughout a 30-year history, we evolved from being an agency that worked primarily with entrepreneurial start-up clients to being an agency that worked with Fortune 500 corporate clients. The transformation occurred for several reasons. We were successful with several entrepreneurial start-ups, so it becomes a natural evolution of a maturing company. But we helped the natural evolution along because we quickly learned that corporate clients were much better at paying their bills than entrepreneurs. We had several entrepreneurial clients who routinely wanted to debate which parts of their billing they would pay and which parts they wouldn't pay. We had made good on our deliverables to these clients, but they perhaps believed we used a different route to accomplish our goals, which in some entrepreneurial minds opened up the billing for negotiation. It is a part of that entrepreneurial spirit to dicker. In our experience, corporate clients almost never wanted to negotiate their billing, and, if they did question it, it was most often because of an honest mistake and it was a reasonable request.

Our evolution was also driven by iconic brands attracting similar iconic brands. We had demonstrated accomplishments by showing work from Budweiser and Betty Crocker, making the agency more appealing to brands such as State Farm Insurance and Hershey's. It is also true that when you work with well-known, iconic brands, many entrepreneurs assume you are too expensive and do not pursue the relationship further.

The Failure Factor

Raise your sights. Rather than aim at a mark you know you cannot miss, set your sights on a goal worth achieving that entails some risk of failure.

Ovation had to learn how to work differently with corporate America. There are always exceptions to the rule, but, in general, corporate clients don't want to be the first one on the block to try something new and untested. You can often get entrepreneurs excited about testing new ideas by simply telling them they'd be the first to ever attempt to grow their business using this idea. When corporate clients hear they will be the first to try an idea, they are stopped dead in their tracks. I can hear the year-end employee performance review now: "You mean you had no evidence this new idea would work? You were just going on your gut instinct that it was somehow a good idea?" They don't want to be first. Truth be told, in most cases, they're probably not wild about being the second one in the pool either. They like it when they can look at a track record of successful ideas before they jump in with both feet. So when new, riskier, growing-the-business ideas were rejected by corporate America, we quickly learned to present the ideas surrounded with historical data and case studies from other companies that had already successfully used the idea, even if we had to stretch to make the connection. We also made it a point to keep several entrepreneurial accounts in the client mix, as they were more willing to try new, edgy ideas. In addition, the agency used edgier advertising campaigns that showcased more "out there" case studies. The combination of these initiatives made it more acceptable for more conservative corporate clients to take the leap with a so-called risky advertising idea.

Corporate clients wisely required some kind of pro forma or return on investment (ROI) analysis, which Ovation embraced as a permanent philosophy, no matter the kind of client we worked with. It is good discipline to take the knowledge you have acquired from a lifetime of work with a variety of clients and project it onto a spreadsheet, thereby predicting how business would react to a new idea for a specific client.

Whether you are an ad agency or a leader within a company, part of your job is to continue to add value. One way to add value is with regular "client growth meetings" that focus on studying past results—both successes and failures—to aid in determining future directions. If this idea worked for company Y, then perhaps a variation of that idea might lead us to test another new idea for the company. Or often it can be profitable to review winning and losing marketing results across different companies and predict how other companies will perform with a test campaign. The goal is to stay on the edge, always adding value to the work you are providing.

Sometimes your ideas will succeed. That is the easy part, as everyone loves and supports a proven winner, and the inspirational adrenaline just flows. Life is good and profits abound.

Sometimes your ideas will fail, which will add valuable knowledge to your database of ideas and oftentimes inspire you to refine the idea and try again. Companies need to remain open to the possibilities that reasonable ideas need consideration and room to breathe and develop, and, yes, sometimes fail.

In some ways, analyzing failure is even tougher than stepping up and taking risks, but if you can master analyzing your failures as easily as you roll out of bed, you can make huge improvements in the way you execute your work.

If you are confident in who you are and the knowledge that failure is a good thing, you should be able to learn from and discuss your failures with the same detachment you would use to discuss what you could do to improve the dinner you cooked last evening.

CHAPTER INSIGHTS
Step-by-Step or One Gigantic Leap?

- **Set a stretch goal.** A stretch goal is one that you know you will probably not achieve—at least on your first attempt. However, the gains you make may surprise you when compared to setting a goal you know you can achieve. For example, if you walk regularly for your daily exercise, it's no stretch to sign up for a 5K or 10K community event. To stretch your abilities, sign up for a half-marathon or one that will require disciplined training and commitment. Another stretch goal could be to master a foreign language rapidly by totally immersing yourself in the culture through native speakers, books, newspapers, audiotapes, restaurants, movies, ethnic community events, or travel.

- **Try something new.** Make it a habit to try one new activity, sport, or experience every month. It doesn't matter what it is—rock climbing, painting, baking bread, tennis, experimental theater, or whatever appeals to you. You will likely fail at some things and succeed at others, but either way you will learn from the experience.

- **Try something old.** Take a failed idea or project. Examine it for insights into why it failed. Was there a particular time when it went off course? What factors contributed to its failure? If circumstances were different, might it succeed? Knowing what you know now, how confident would you be in trying it again?

*Note

You can read Dean Karnazes's full interview, "The Dean Machine," by Katie Arnold in the January 2007 issue of *Outside* magazine on the its Website: *http://outside.away.com/outside/bodywork/200701/new-years-resolutions-2.html*.

12

Break a Rib

If you're willing to examine failure and to look not just at your outward physical performance, but your internal workings, too, losing can be valuable.

—Lance Armstrong, seven-time winner of the Tour de France

I own four bicycles. That might sound like a lot, but each bike has a special feature or purpose, not unlike the variety of specialty clubs many golfers carry around in their bags.

For many years, I purchased most of my bikes, accessories, and service at one particular bike shop. I was a loyal customer, but one day I had a disagreement with them. To start things off, they returned my bike to me and failed to correctly tighten down the skewer on the back wheel, which keeps the wheel firmly on the bike. The first time I went for a ride the wheel came off. When the wheel came off the bike, so did I. I went down hard, broke a rib, and removed numerous patches of skin from my body. I have to date broken 13 ribs in biking accidents, and it is an unpleasant experience. An apology would have gone a long way to solving the problem—I can be extremely forgiving—but none was ever offered.

Soon after the bike crash, I decided to sell an older bike I had purchased from the same bike shop. They agreed to help me with the sale. After selling my bike they told me about their policy to take a 20-percent commission for selling used equipment. Certainly not an unreasonable policy when communicated in advance, but when communicated after selling the bike of a longtime loyal customer with a healing rib, it is not a smart policy. But I can be loyal and forgiving.

A month or two went by, and it occurred to me that the bike shop had not given me a check for the bike they sold for me. When I asked about the check for selling the bike, they then informed me they had issued me a store credit for selling the bike. Again, not an entirely unreasonable policy—if only this had been shared with me prior to my selling the bike. This was all adding up now, on top of the 20-percent commission and after they had broken my rib.

Next, I had some work done on one of my bikes, and requested they deliver the bike to me at the office with a new spare tire in the bike bag. When I went to take my bike for a ride, there was no spare tire. The mechanic who delivered the bike claimed it was there when he left it. I could not help but wonder if the mechanic who dropped off the spare tire was the same one who was supposed to lock down the back wheel on my bike!

As a customer, I was getting irritated.

When I received my next bill from the bike shop, there was a charge listed for handlebars that I had purchased. I remembered seeing the handlebars in bike catalogs for considerably less money. When I inquired about this, I was told that, while I was charged a higher price, I was not charged for the installation of these items on my bike. Once again, not an entirely unreasonable arrangement, but after the broken rib, the 20-percent commission, the store credit, the lost tire, and the reasonable yet poorly communicated installation pricing strategy, I was done. The marriage was over. The relationship ended with a thud, and I moved on to a better bike shop and started an outstanding new relationship.

I love to shop at the bike store, and do so most of the time because I like their equipment. I am a loyal customer, but do not *make* me shop at your bike store, because then I am no longer in control of the situation and it is no longer my decision to shop there. Create a store, or a company, that is so good I feel compelled to spend my money with you.

When you do, I am making the decision to buy at your store, which is far stronger than you making me shop there.

I cannot help but draw some analogies to my own business experience and the customer service we gave our clients. I must admit we had similar communication problems with clients because we just didn't have the guts to properly communicate a pricing strategy, or at times we created advertising that didn't perform as we had hoped—similar to not tightening the skewer and the resulting broken rib.

Putting myself in the bike shop owner's shoes, I asked, "Was the bike shop reasonable, or was the customer's expectation or reaction unreasonable?" The answer is easy. The bike shop doesn't define what is right or what is wrong, and neither do any of us. Our customers define if they are treated fairly. If customers believe they are being treated unfairly, then any business faces a nearly impossible challenge in attempting to change that perception.

> ### The Failure Factor
> Expect some pain. Risk and opportunity go hand in hand; getting hurt is sometimes part of the game. Take your lumps—and prizes—and keep moving forward.

CHAPTER INSIGHTS
Reasonable Expectations

- **What are the options?** Considering my own experience as a customer, what did I expect the bike shop could have done differently?

  First, the owner of the bike shop should have called and said he had just learned about my broken rib and that he was truly sorry it had happened. A simple apology would have gone a long way to help ease the tension (and the pain). Lesson: When we mess up, somebody must make that call or visit. When it is serious enough, that someone should be the president—I have made such calls many times. I keep kneepads at my office specifically for such occasions.

Second, the bike shop did not communicate well regarding its standard policies. Customers do not mind reasonable charges, but they hate surprises, and they hate being told of a charge after the fact.

Lesson: If something is going to cost more, call in advance and tell the customer so he or she is in control of the situation and can make the decision to spend the money or not.

Finally, do not force a customer to do business with you by creating one-sided policies that give the customer no freedom of choice.

Lesson: Create a company with which people truly want to be involved for the long haul. Let's foster relationships with our customers that benefit us both. Let's be certain that customers know they are going to be treated fairly. Let's be focused on selling our customers the best products and services that contribute to their long-term success—not just our own.

13

Winning and Losing the Negotiation Game

My father said, "You must never try to make all the money that's in a deal. Let the other fellow make some money too, because if you have a reputation for always making all the money, you won't have many deals."
—J. Paul Getty

One of my ad agency's clients for many years was insurance giant State Farm. We weren't initially hired by their regular marketing people but by the people who were responsible for getting insurance agents to use the co-op advertising funds that State Farm made available to their agents. State Farm's statistics showed that the agents weren't spending the dollars available to them, and it was a generous co-op program that the agents should have been all over. State Farm's agency of 20-plus years was the global juggernaut DDB. (DDB is one of the leading agencies in the world, with 2008 revenues exceeding $12 billion and 200 offices around the world.) Because of this, the co-op advertising unit of State Farm was granted special permission to work with our small agency in La Crosse, Wisconsin, mainly because the nice folks in co-op advertising felt DDB had not paid enough attention to their program. As assignments go, it wasn't the most glamorous account Ovation Marketing had ever won, but we viewed it as a great opportunity to work with the biggest insurance company in the country. And as the old sales saying goes, "Penetrate and radiate." We thought that, given sufficient time, we could explore other advertising opportunities. Little did we know at the time that we were caught up in the internal politics of old and established relationships at State Farm. There was the "old guard" marketing department that had deep, personal ties to DDB and wanted to retain that exclusive relationship, and frankly didn't want any part of some new agency with a funny first name. Then there was the "new guard" that wanted change.

In the end—I'm not making this up—they opted for the King Solomon solution and proposed cutting the country in half and giving Ovation one half and DDB the other half. Neither DDB nor Ovation stepped forward and objected to cutting the country in half, as the real mother did in the famous biblical version when King Solomon proposed cutting the child in half, thus positioning the agency that didn't want the country cut in half as "the more concerned ad agency." For either Ovation or DDB to proclaim that cutting the program in half would not be in the best interests of State Farm would have been a bold and interesting gamble that may or may not have paid off, perhaps giving the agency who appeared the more concerned the whole country and budget, rather than half of the country and corresponding budget. Sadly, neither agency will ever know what the outcome might have been, as we both reluctantly agreed to take half, a classic case of neither agency having the balls to go for all or nothing. I'm not sure anyone at State Farm would have made the mental connection to King Solomon and awarded all of the work to one agency, but I have added it to my list of decisions I wish I had made, as entrepreneurs are gamblers at heart. And what a bold gamble that would have been, as the account was worth about $2 million a year to us, for seven years, or $14 million. But had they been moved by our concern not to split the country in half and awarded us DDB's half of the pie as a reward, it would have been worth an additional $14 million to us, for a total of $28 million. On the other hand, had they said, "You're right; we shouldn't divide the country in half, so we are giving it all to DDB," we would have received nothing. That is one of the reasons why I love coming to work. How often do you get to contemplate a $28 million bet? "Balls," said the queen. "If I had them I'd be king."

DDB did not like another agency moving in on their long-term iconic account, but we had to work together at establishing parameters for the program, and everyone played together surprisingly well. Ovation was hardly a threat to their global dominance.

Because it was such an unusual assignment for an ad agency, we negotiated a flat hourly rate for our time involved in helping the agents or placing the media buys. Plus, if we needed to buy any outside services to aid the agents in determining how to spend their co-op dollars, we would bill that at our cost to State Farm. It seemed like a fair deal to all involved at the time. The relationship flourished for years, and the agents' use of co-op dollars dramatically increased both under our direction and the other half of the country that DDB controlled. Both agencies were successful, and after six years of a great working relationship State Farm decided to pull the program from the nice co-op advertising folks that hired us, and instead had us report to the sharks in their marketing department. Yes, that same marketing department that opposed hiring the new outside agency all those years ago. The warning bells went off immediately in my head. The beginning of the end started with their immediate objection to the contract we had negotiated. They felt we had somehow taken advantage of the nice folks who hired us. It certainly wasn't the first thing you wanted to hear when you were trying to manage a new relationship. It wasn't as though we had held a gun to anyone's head to get them to sign the contract they had renewed six times. Ovation eventually lost the State Farm

> ### The Failure Factor
>
> Know your limits. Negotiating or taking a calculated risk requires advance knowledge and planning. Do your homework so you can recognize the signs leading to dead ends.

business, but I am certain it wasn't because we had negoti-ated a contract that was too beneficial in our favor. All good things come to an end, including agency-client relationships. It is the way of the world, as business needs constantly change and evolve. The day you win the business is also the first day you start losing the business.

Client contract negotiations are always interesting. Gen-erally the ad agency does not deal from a position of strength due to the nature of the relationship. The client is typically interviewing five or six agencies that are each panting like hungry dogs to obtain the agency-of-record assignment. We've never been in a position in which we interviewed five or six of the largest insurance companies and then called and informed them whose advertising we have decided to create. That would be a fun and exciting new twist to obtain-ing new business, and is about as likely as a camel passing through the eye of a needle. From time to time, in the annals of rare advertising occurrences, there have been two or three red-hot creative shops for which two or three clients have fought for their services, but you can count those examples on one hand in the past 50 years, and have a number of fingers left over.

When we began contract negotiations, we were made painfully aware that we went to unusual lengths to deliver the best creative, and we were over-the-top passionate about our service. That combination assured that we were almost never the low bidder.

The basic bottom-line premise of cost negotiations is simi-lar in that most companies want to charge as much as pos-sible for their product or service, and the purchaser most often attempts to pay as little as possible. Frankly, negotiat-ing is a game. The better you play the game, the more money you make. This is the game our agency played with our cli-ents and our suppliers. We kept positioning ourselves in a way that allowed us to receive top dollar for our services, while our clients brought us off that position. If they were successful in getting us to reduce our price, we made less money. If we were successful in holding ground, we made more money. It's that simple.

To win at the negotiation game, a service-oriented company must momentarily disassociate itself from the usual "can-do" attitude—the attitude of always saying yes to client requests.

For example, let's say a client had asked, "Our supplier in Taiwan just raised our fabric prices. We know you are scheduled to send the final files to the printer tomorrow, so would it be possible for you to change and raise all the prices in the catalog by 10 percent?"

Our answer would have been: "Yes, we can do that for you, even if we have to stay up all night to get it done! You are our client and you need our help. We will jump through flaming hoops to help you in this situation."

But let's say the client asked, "We didn't budget enough money for this catalog. Can you help us out and produce it for 15 percent less than your normal rate?"

After exhausting all reasonable attempts to work more efficiently (which good companies should routinely do to stay competitive), our answer had to be, "No. We're sorry. We cannot simply cut our rates. We must maintain a profit to stay in business so we can continue to hire the best and the brightest talent who work every day, bringing value to your account. We work on a very modest profit margin. If we reduce our rates, we will be unable to stay in business, and then we would be of absolutely no service to you. Perhaps we could look at reducing the number of pages in the catalog and put that saved money into creative costs? Or perhaps we could look at modifying or reducing some of our services in hopes of saving you 15 percent." We needed to be accommodating in trying to help them with their problem, but we could not simply say yes and take the hit, or we would shortly be out of business.

Long-term clients respect that a business must make a profit, and understand that if the business is strong it can serve them better. From time to time companies must take on short-term, one-time projects from clients who are not particularly concerned about a mutually beneficial, long-term relationship. They are most often interested in paying as little as possible, and coincidentally they are most often in a hurry. So if you want the work, it becomes a game that must be played regarding the price. These are the types of clients that should, ideally, pay a premium price because of their short-term and often demanding nature.

How have I developed such a cold, callous business attitude? Because presidents become accustomed to a steady stream of people they work with reminding them in one way or another that they would prefer an ever-increasing salary and profit sharing, a higher-valued company, better health insurance, faster computers, bigger pipes, better wiring, new software, more education, more seminars, new BlackBerries, more parking spaces, the latest computer toys, and so on. Frankly, it is satisfying to deliver on their needs. It's the best part of my job. I give someone a raise or a performance bonus (that they have earned), and together we share a moment of success. I can't wait until we can do it again. It is how I keep score. Or, if I tell the IT department that we have the money to purchase bigger, faster computers, their eyes light up like pinball machines. It's addicting to them and to me. It's a habit I want to continue, and to do that, the business needs to continue to make a profit and charge a fair price for our services.

Good negotiation skills can also benefit you personally, as one should always make an effort to negotiate a better price. I was recently doing some gift shopping and found the perfect item. I got so excited I almost blurted out, "I'll take it." I wanted it badly and the price looked more than reasonable. But then I remembered, *Oh yeah, I've got to play the negotiation game.* I know many people hate to negotiate and proudly proclaim they are not good at it. I think negotiation fears are unfounded as negotiation is an easy and simple process we should all practice whenever the opportunity arises.

So I took a deep breath and stood back and studied the object I desperately wanted carefully and slowly with dramatic emphasis in full view of the salesperson. I opened and then closed the door of the object. I had a little problem closing the door tightly, which made me study the door more carefully, as if the sticky door presented a major roadblock to the deal. I said nothing, as I know I am not an Academy Award–winning actor. I slowly and carefully studied the object again and made a concerned "hmmm" noise. Then I implemented my ruthless negotiation strategy and pointed to the sticker price and said quietly, "Can you do any better than this?"

"Sure!" the more-than-eager salesperson blurted out as he went over to the calculator and reduced the price by 42 percent—thereby saving me several hundred dollars! In my haste and excitement I had almost paid full price. That is most often all it takes to successfully negotiate.

CHAPTER INSIGHTS
There's Always Something to Negotiate

- **Know your worth.** Most businesses will cut their prices when someone politely asks their people if they can sharpen their pencils. Asking them to put the price in writing, as if you've decided to get four or five competitive bids, can have the same effect. A written quote is a significant reminder.

- **Play nice.** You don't need to be ruthless or mean to negotiate. In fact, oftentimes, the nicer you are the more effectively it works. It doesn't take great skill or guts to be a successful negotiator. Use a little patience; a couple of well-placed "hmmms" or "I see," and the money will flow right into your pocket or your company coffers.

- **Bide your time.** Did you ever notice most sales-oriented companies have a special that is ending within days or hours? Guess what? They will have a new special shortly after that one ends, and it might be better than the one that is about to expire. If I had a dollar for each time I was about to make a major equipment purchase and they told me the special was about to end, I'd have about $74! It happens a lot!

14

Never Threaten to Quit Anything

Never quit. It is the easiest cop-out in the world.
Set a goal and don't quit until you attain it.
When you do attain it, set another goal, and
don't quit until you reach it. Never quit.

—Bear Bryant

One of my associates at Ovation was once engaged in a dispute with a company that had provided services that fell far short of expectations, and we were trying to obtain a refund. My mild-mannered associate, who is an active volunteer in her church, volunteered to handle the negotiations. I was relieved, as dealing with a supplier of questionable ethics is one of my least favorite things to do. I was happy to stand back and let her work her magic. Plus, she was good at collections and always engaged them with a smile on her face and a can-do, compromising attitude.

I checked back on our church volunteer several months later, and her language regarding the supplier had transformed from that of an angel on high to that of a plumber (with all due respect to the plumbing industry). She was calm, cool, and collected when I had last left her. Then I ran across this line in an e-mail she had sent to our former supplier of questionable ethics:

"Supplier's name [with no salutation]: This is not acceptable. We are not accustomed to, and WILL NOT work with, vendors that lie and try to deceive us."

Wow! We had degenerated into some strong, non-collaborative, non-problem-solving language. "What happened?" I asked. How had the rhetoric reached such a high confrontational level, as this was clearly not her usual negotiating technique? In the heat of the battle, this supplier had tweaked her so often and jerked her around so much, she lost a bit of her usual calm and cool collection style.

I have seen it happen time and again to people in a position of leadership, including yours truly. The bad guys wear you down and get on your nerves during negotiations. The rhetoric continues to escalate until it is out of control. Neither party can see the other's point of view, and the possibility of collaborating on an agreement disappears. Certainly there are times when one of the parties' behavior is so egregious that there is no hope or reason to compromise. But in most cases, we are wise to find common ground upon which we can put together a face-saving deal for both parties. If I can keep legal fees for solving such problems near zero, I am elated. I am also motivated by the outstanding advice I received after one of my problem-solving failures resulted in the necessity to engage legal counsel: "If you get in a pissing match with a skunk, you will most certainly get skunk urine on your body." That simple sentence has an amazing impact on my desire to compromise.

I served as president of a nonprofit land conservancy for five years. We had a long-standing agreement with our city to purchase land atop the bluffs overlooking the Mississippi River. Each year the city would allocate money to make land purchases, and we would use that money to get matching state grants, doubling and even tripling the city's investment. It was an important part of the work we did. The agreement had been in effect for almost 10 years, but it had to be renegotiated at periodic intervals. This was one of those times. Our executive director was getting jerked around ad nauseam by the city attorney in the negotiations. The city would put things in the contract, then take them out, and then reintroduce them without highlighting any of the changes. They were driving our people crazy. (They then slipped in a clause that was so vaguely worded it sounded as though our little nonprofit land conservancy would indemnify the big city for the life of the contract.) It was a relationship that we valued, and we were careful to be kind and respectful to those in the government who were making this deal happen for us. But by now the negotiations had dragged on for months, the current agreement had expired, both sides were getting irritated, the rhetoric was starting to escalate, and the relationship was deteriorating. Here is the missile we fired at the assistant city attorney in the heat of battle:

> I do not see how a small, nonprofit organization like MVC [Mississippi Valley Conservancy] is supposed to agree to pay all of the city's attorney fees that might arise in one of the many legal disputes the city gets in with neighboring municipalities. This is especially troubling given that the city has used language so broad that if MVC merely 'contributes to' the city's inability to comply with the records law, MVC is supposed to pay *all* of the city's attorney fees. That means the city could be primarily at fault for a breach of the public records law, but the city would still be able to shift all of the expense to MVC.
>
> The added language is a deal-breaker. Please remove that language and reinstate the language in the version above. Otherwise, I think MVC will have no option but to withdraw participation.

How had we reached the point at which we were now threatening the city that had supported us so strongly? What happened to something like: "I certainly understand why you feel the city should be indemnified, but a small nonprofit like ours simply doesn't have the money to take such a position. We wish we could as that would resolve this problem we are so interested in solving with you."—or some such wording that keeps the aura of compromise in the air, rather than threatening to end or quit the relationship. In the end we did embrace a spirit of compromise and completed the deal.

After a long, internal dialogue with myself many years ago, I agreed that I would never threaten to quit anything, and I have kept my promise. Threatening to quit limits your options, and quitting takes them right down to zero. I have been tempted a million times to quit or threaten to quit a host of things. There is something about threatening to quit that is alluring. It feels macho, bold, and decisive in its action. It puts finality to the negotiations that you now find incredibly irritating.

But when you quit, there is no more compromise, the game is over. It is often a testosterone-filled event. It is the ultimate statement, as you have effectively told that person to stick it where the sun never shines. You have made the definitive statement that, "Yes, asshole, I can live without you. Here; I'll prove it. Go screw yourself. I quit. I am taking my marble game somewhere else." (It even feels good to type it now during this demonstrative simulation.) You feel so strongly about your dispute that you are willing to walk away from the negotiations, or the game, or the deal, or whatever it is you just quit or threatened to quit.

Don't do it. Quitting is a slippery slope. It starts a pattern in life that is hard to break.

I have a good friend who routinely quits bike races when it is apparent he is going to expend a lot of energy and not win. His thinking is that he can quit, save the energy he would have expended losing, and come back tomorrow and fight another day, stronger for the energy he saved. I understand his thinking, but it terrifies me, and I would never adopt it as my strategy for fear of the precedent it sets. I've averaged 15 cycling, running, or triathlon races a year for the past 30 years, and I have never quit one race, as I am fearful that the next time I am in a race that is extremely hot and uncomfortable, or a strong competitor is continuously ratcheting up the aerobic pain to unbearable levels, or I am nauseated from the hard efforts I'm putting in just to stay with the lead pack, or any combination of other painful events that occur during intense competition, I will scream, "I quit!"

There is a point during most intense competitive events where those little voices come and sit on your shoulder and tell you that you are weak and it would be much more comfortable to stop and grab a cold refreshment and sit over there under that shade tree. Winning is a habit, and so is quitting, in business or sport.

Churchill summed it up best: *"Never, never, never give up!"*

The number of races I have won outright in my life can be counted on one hand, and I would still have one or two fingers left. The few times I was out in front were each an incredibly exhilarating feeling. You are so pumped up because you are leading; the adrenaline is pulsing through your body, and the experience feels effortless. When running, it feels as though your feet are off the ground. When cycling, it feels as though you are flying downhill with the wind at your back. Whatever drug your body is producing should be illegal, because you are so high you have an unbelievably unfair advantage over your competitors. Winning in business is the same way. When your company is out front on a new business pitch, you are flying. Everything seems to come your way. Even mistakes can be magically transformed into positive events with the right words here or there.

The Failure Factor

You must finish to fail. Finishing means you've given it your all; even if you fail, you've done your best. If you quit, you've given up.

The question is: How do you bring back that can-do winning attitude to the business negotiation table? Where do you find the confidence and swagger that you had before the process of negotiation wore you down and stole your compromising spirit?

It is hard work to maintain a welcoming and compromising attitude, but maintain it you must. Keep in mind that negotiations are not personal, and it is merely a game to see who is most skillful at negotiation. Those who play the game best usually walk away with the most money or the best contract or whatever the winning booty happens to be. As soon as you feel your language become confrontational, focus on turning it positive and "can-do."

CHAPTER INSIGHTS
Negotiate to the Very End

- **Cuban Missile Crisis bargaining.** One of my favorite negotiation tools is what I affectionately call the "Cuban Missile Crisis" bargaining technique. It is yet one more way to snatch success from impending failure. During the Cuban Missile Crisis of the 1960s, the United States received two very different and conflicting offers from the Soviet Union. One of the offers was extremely confrontational and unforgiving to U.S. interests, whereas the other offer, through a different channel, was conciliatory and compromising. President Kennedy chose to ignore the confrontational offer and graciously, outwardly, vocally, and warmly embraced the compromising offer. And it worked. The Russians blinked and Kennedy achieved one of the biggest victories of his brief administration.

  I have used a variation of that approach by graciously, outwardly, vocally, and warmly embracing an adversary's latest offer, and then quietly remarking that we did have to modify two or three words that, of course, turn the negotiation slightly in our favor. But they are relieved by the heightened state in which we emote our enthusiasm for their offer, and, like us, they too are anxious to put an end to the negotiations.

- **Care, but not that much.** Perhaps the best negotiation tip I ever received came from author Herb Cohen, who said, "You've got to care, but not that much." In an ad agency loaded with over-performing Type A personalities who cared about everything, the phrase often became a saving mantra during tough negotiations when we loved a creative approach, but a client was less than enthusiastic. "You've got to care, but not that much" allows you to let go, or at least loosen your grip on a good idea or a negotiation position, when it is no longer prudent to sell it or support it. Certain things simply won't go your way during negotiations, and you must let go and keep the bigger end goal in mind.

- **Walk away.** You can walk away from tough negotiations, and oftentimes must, but it is best to do so by not threatening to quit. Walking away is a tool of last resort. Even then, it is better to just walk than threaten to walk. Threatening to quit or walk is like whining, which is not an admired trait in our society. It sends up red flags to your adversary that you are weak and playing your last card. It becomes more difficult to continue proposing alternative solutions once you have said you are going to quit if you don't get your way. Plus, once you threaten to quit and then don't quit, you have lost all credibility. It is like the parent who continues to threaten the child with some dire punishment and never follows through. The child quickly learns it is yet another idle threat, and the parent loses credibility. It is actually far stronger to imply and hint that, alas, you are running out of alternatives, and then sadly announce, with much regret, that you have no other viable alternatives, but don't utter the final words, as it ends the negotiations.

15
Answer the Question, Please

*When you cannot make up your mind
between two evenly balanced courses
of action, choose the bolder.*
—W.J. Slim

New business pitches are the lifeblood of any ad agency and most businesses. If after a loss, we learned from our mistakes, moved on, and started winning more, then the learning experience and the loss were worth it. It was a worthwhile investment in our continuing education and constant improvement.

We once lost an agency shootout because we failed to answer a direct question: "Where would you take our brand in the future?" We simply failed to step up and answer the question as succinctly as we should have. It was a painful experience because brand positioning was one of the things we loved most and did best.

In business, when someone asks you a direct question, you must answer it directly, immediately, clearly, and in sufficient detail to satisfy your questioner. As a follow-up, after you believe you've nailed the answer, you should say, "Did I answer your question to your satisfaction?" If the questioner says no, or wants more detail, you are still in the game because you can recover from your first failure and keep going until he or she assures you that, yes, you did indeed nail it. Then you can celebrate.

Even the speed at which you answer the question can have an impact on your future credibility and the perception your inquisitor has of your capabilities. Let's say I'm talking to a potential client who wants to market an energy bar. An early and typical question the client might ask would be, "What experience does your agency have with marketing in the food and beverage category?" Throughout a 30-year time span Ovation worked with more than a dozen food- and beverage-related clients, but if I suddenly drew a blank, or took time to pause and think, it would appear that we had little or no experience. If, however, I quickly responded, "Yes, we've worked with many iconic food and beverage brands, including Hershey's, General Mills, Smucker's, Anheuser-Busch, Sargento Cheese, and others. I'd be happy to provide a complete list and samples of the work we created for each of these brands." Truth be told, I kept cheat sheets all over my office because I have never had total and rapid recall and didn't care to lose the sale as I gathered my thoughts. In our society we are judged quickly, and if we slip or pause with our answers to direct questions, the relationship can be over before it begins.

Answering questions directly becomes especially true when coming face to face with the "hunt/kill" mentality of the typical Type A corporate executive. I confess: I am a card-carrying member of this group. I possess the hunt/kill mentality on most issues—it is programmed into my DNA. When I ask a question, I expect a direct answer; that is why I asked the question in the first place. I value your opinion, and I want to hear it—now. The sooner you give me the answer, the better and the happier I will be—and the bolder you will appear in my mind. Many people are weak at answering questions directly because of our old friend, fear of failure. Answering a question directly requires a commitment to a firm answer. Some feel it is safer to hedge their bet and dance around a subject with talk of options, possibilities, and potential outcomes.

"So, tell me, Bill. If we give you the assignment to create our Website, when can we expect the site to go live?" That is a typical question that makes agencies hesitate, as no one wants to over- or under-promise on such a crucial detail. And so we began a bizarre verbal dance. "Well, we'll need to get the team together and determine the needs of your organization, write a requirements document for the site, then a functions document, talk to some of your customers to address usability issues, build the wireframes..." and on and on. What the Type A corporate executive wanted to hear was, "A Website like the one your business desires typically takes eight to 12 months. We can give you a more precise timetable after you hire us."

But, to steal shamelessly from Machiavelli, nothing is more delicate, nor more dangerous to conduct, nor more doubtful of success than to step up as leader and take a firm stand regarding the price of anything. There is a school of thought that it is almost bad manners to talk about the cost of a product or service in mixed company. If you look at a hundred typical Microsoft PowerPoint presentations in which someone is selling something to someone else, 99.9 percent of them will place the cost at the end of the presentation. It appears to be certain suicide to start your presentation with the price. I always wanted to move the cost to the front of the presentation just to stand out and be different or see if anyone would actually die from the experience. I've actually seen companies excuse some of the people in the presentation "before we actually start talking about money and the costs to get this project done." It's as though these people would somehow melt if they learned what we actually charged for our hard work.

So if a potential client asked, "How much will this brochure cost?" they often received a long oratory about the price of paper and postage, finding the right printer, and so on. At the end they may have heard something along the lines of, "We should be able to get the work completed at a reasonable cost." Oftentimes, there was no direct answer to the question.

I have watched this phenomenon with my own associates when I ask a routine question: "Do you think we should switch to the new XYZ software?" Again, it requires a relatively easy yes-or-no answer, and, if they so choose, an explanation as to why they are making the recommendation. The explanation is optional, but not mandatory, as I didn't ask for an explanation. I simply asked a yes-or-no question. Yet much of the time I get a long explanation about the benefits of the old versus the new, but no direct answer to my question. Most people who do this are not even aware that they are consciously avoiding taking a firm stand. Explanations are fine, but what is most important is that you make the commitment and answer the initial question that was asked by an extremely focused and time-sensitive executive or client.

"So, tell me, Jane, how many hours will it take for us to finish this project?" Numerical questions are right up there with money questions, as they require not only precise answers, but estimations, which, by nature, leave more room for error.

"Well, Ralph, I've given that a lot of thought."

That is good, I think to myself. *I would hate to think you just pulled the number out of your ass as I do much of the time.*

Jane continues, "If we can get the client to get us the material we need in the next week, I will then need to line up the right team..." and on and on with the explanation. In addition to the fear of commitment that is permeating the air, the dance also continues because it is damn-near impossible to accurately predict how many hours it will take to get anything done on a large project with hundreds of uncontrollable variables. Yet business demands an estimate, even though this presentation may be the first time we have dealt with this particular client and are not familiar with the way they work with their suppliers. We are set up for failure by the very nature of the question. Thus we fear answering it— unless we have been schooled in the belief that it is nobler to be bold and decisive because we know that companies need estimates to plan their project times and allocate resources appropriately. It is a tough job, but someone has to take a stand and come up with an acceptable estimate.

What I really want to hear from Jane in answer to my question is, "Given what we know now, I estimate it will take us 1,200 hours over a six-week period, and here is why I believe it will take that amount of time." But seldom do people simply provide the numerical answer to your question first and *then* support it with evidence.

Answering direct questions is an issue at every company. I had a lawyer on a conference call recently, discussing a complex legal problem. (There should be a special place in heaven or somewhere for lawyers.) We were wrapping up after a long meeting in

The Failure Factor

Listen. Pay attention to the people, the signs, the words, and the surrounding environment to pick up on the cues to guide your response and behavior.

which the lawyer concluded by giving us the choice of two options. I then asked the lawyer, "If you were in our position, would you choose option A or option B?" The lawyer went into a long speech leaning more toward option A than option B, but in no way, shape, or form did the lawyer even come close to answering my direct question.

"You didn't answer the question," I said, as politely as I possibly could, knowing instantly I was going to include this particular discussion in my book, and I desperately wanted to portray myself as thoughtful and caring in my own story. "Would you recommend we do option A or B?" This time the lawyer replied with a shorter speech, recapping in an abbreviated version exactly what had been said in the initial and longer explanation, but still not answering the question about recommending A or B.

So I politely repeated the question a third time and received a 10-second recap followed by the specific answer: "I would choose option A if I were in your position." It took guts and I know I made our lawyer friend extremely uncomfortable by asking her to take a firm stand and make a commitment. It took away her ability to cover her ass or to ever be able to say, "Well, I never specifically said you should choose option A." People simply feel safer couching their arguments in evasive generalizations and not giving an answer.

I noticed that, after the agency shootout in which we didn't answer the question directly, we made positive strides toward conquering the habit of not delivering a direct answer.

Change is hard, and making a commitment is enhanced by the absence of a fear of failure. I know it's hard to break long-held habits—I have a truckload I try to change every day. Changing habits takes self-confidence and a no-fear approach to answering questions directly. People, especially executive decision-makers, value your opinion and they want to hear it; otherwise they simply wouldn't ask for it.

As a leader, it's my responsibility to prove to the people gutsy enough to stick their necks out and provide direct answers that the company will support their answers—even when those answers turn out to be wrong. As a leader, I always reward risk-takers. At Ovation it was no accident that those who took risks and answered questions directly were among the highest paid.

CHAPTER INSIGHTS
A or B?

- **First, the answer.** Answer the immediate question, then provide supporting information. (This is the inverted pyramid style of communication.) If you provide the answer first, the listener can focus on the additional information without the interference of frustration caused by waiting for the answer.

- **Be prepared.** If you're offering a client or executive decision-maker a choice of options, weigh the pros and cons ahead of time and go into the meeting with a clear recommendation for the optimal solution and the rationale to back it up.

- **Use your experience.** When asked for numbers or dates, draw on your experience or others' experiences to provide best estimates based on known facts or similar projects. Provide a range, margin of error, or confidence ranking behind your numbers, if needed, when facts are scarce or subject to change.

16

Anaerobic Creativity

Excellence is an art won by training and habituation. We do not act rightly because we have virtue or excellence, but we rather have those because we have acted rightly. We are what we repeatedly do. Excellence, then, is not an act but a habit.

—Aristotle

I believe strongly in the many positive health claims that are made about exercise and believe that associates who exercise regularly are indeed more creative than their sedentary counterparts. I also believe that people who exercise regularly are better problem-solvers, stay more relaxed under pressure, are happier, contribute to lower healthcare costs, are more well-rounded, and, last but not least, are healthier and miss work far less often than non-exercisers. I have experienced strong statistical proof for many of these beliefs.

At Ovation we provided a first-class, on-site exercise facility, and also gave associates free memberships to health club facilities within our city and actively encouraged them to exercise before or after work, during their lunch hour, or any time they could work it into their schedules. All we asked for in return was an honest day's work. They knew when they should be working and when they could be exercising.

We were very creative instilling in our associates the desire to embrace an active lifestyle. One year, we asked associates to select a "stretch goal" involving some type of physical challenge they had never accomplished, which would stretch them beyond their own personal comfort level. If they were physically inactive, we suggested they complete a 5K or 10K walk. If they were already active, they could select events like a 10K run or even a marathon. One person completed a course to earn a black belt in karate. Two women selected a 30-mile bike ride, a distance they had never ridden before. If they completed their stretch goal, they were asked to write a short story about the experience and share it with their associates. Each was then awarded $250 in cash to celebrate their success.* We received a great deal of local and advertising industry media attention for these "innovative" health and exercise policies.

> **The Failure Factor**
>
> Swim against the current. If you're only doing what everyone else is doing, you're missing out on failure—and success—opportunities. Be unique. Stretch yourself and the envelope.

Frankly, I am amazed at the reaction I get from my business-leader peers in the business community. For a relatively minor financial investment in the health and wellness of the people who work their hearts out for me, I am heralded as a forward-thinking visionary who is providing much-needed leadership in an area where most leaders have done little to improve the physical health of their workforce.

Although I enjoy the attention and kind words, I find it undeserving. What is visionary about finding a direct correlation between an increase in an employee's exercise and a dramatic corresponding decrease in sick days? There is a new study out on almost a daily basis supporting the benefits of exercise.

What is visionary about watching associates who exercise regularly stand up day after day to the enormous pressure that work can inflict upon a person's mental and physical well-being, and perform to near perfection?

What is visionary about asking a "stressed out" associate when was the last time he exercised, and finding the not-at-all surprising answer that he hadn't had time to exercise in months?

I don't believe I'm a visionary on the subject of exercise. I am a hard-core capitalist interested in making the most amount of money possible! The correlation between healthy associates and exercise is direct and conclusive. A business owner misses an important opportunity if he or she does *not* recognize the gains a corporation can make by providing its associates with the facilities and incentives to embrace exercise in their lives!

The strangest thing to me is that, if you read *The Wall Street Journal* or *USA Today* on a regular basis, there is a story at least once a week that provides scientific evidence of the benefits of exercise. It has been only in the past few years that the captains of industry have made the correlation between the benefits of exercise and the people who work for them.

I have been encouraging coworkers to exercise since the 1980s—investing corporate funds in the health of the workforce. Perhaps it takes a leader who has personally experienced the health benefits of exercise to best understand the enormous benefits that exercise can provide for the workforce. Sadly, as is the case with most of America, many of our leaders are sedentary and overweight. Therefore, they don't understand how exercise can invigorate and keep a workforce healthy, dramatically improving the creativity of their staff and the success of their companies.

CHAPTER INSIGHTS
Let's Get Physical

- **Get moving.** Providing a physical outlet for stress is the best dollar-for-dollar investment a leader can make in his or her company. Rip off a successful program such as the one I mentioned, or invent one of your own. I spend most warm weather weekends racing on a bike, but I am an aberration, and it is not at all normal or necessary to go over the top with exercise. Studies have proven that all you need do to reap huge benefits is get people to elevate their heart rate for 30 minutes, five times a week. And you don't need large amounts of money to get started.

- **Never underestimate the power of a free T-shirt.** People will do some pretty crazy things for a free T-shirt. And don't be afraid to tell the media what you've done. Health and feature editors go crazy for this kind of story. Your company becomes the focal point as a healthy place to work in your community. That's a nice reputation to have when you need to hire a new receptionist or call on a potential new client. Plus, the media will come back to you again and again each time health is in the news. And there you are, the benevolent health leader who does incredible things for the company's workforce, and all it cost you was a T-shirt. (Sort of. You must also provide an area for your associates to shower after they have exercised. At Ovation we initially built one shower area, but one shower was a bit shortsighted for a family of 40 exercising during the lunch hour, so we ended up building additional shower areas. It was still a small price to pay for good health.)

*Note

Years later, during a routine IRS audit of our company, we were required to report the $250 fitness incentive as ordinary income and pay taxes on the awards, which I and my associates faithfully did. Our government doesn't offer much in the way of incentives that encourage healthy activities on the part of corporations. Imagine the potential positive impact we could have on healthcare costs if exercising incentives were embraced instead of taxed.

17

Continuous Improvement

Something is wrong if associates do not look around each day, find things that are tedious or boring, and then rewrite the procedures. Even last month's manual should be out of date.

—Taiichi Ohno, the father of Toyota Production System

I believe in attacking yourself. I believe in continuous improvement, change, and always seeking a better way to do something. I find it almost inconceivable that a company would not seek ways of doing things better, quicker, or faster. I also think that sometimes you can only take continuous improvement so far, and then you have to "blow it up" and just start all over again from scratch.

There is, however, a downside to continuous improvement. It can occur when you have extremely hardworking and conscientious employees who believe strongly that they have given something their best shot, and they have put their heart and soul into doing it right the first time: They can become completely unglued when you tell them there has to be a better way to do what they just did. It could imply, at least to their way of thinking, that they have done something wrong. The problem arises when you have an employee who does not like to analyze and discuss mistakes. It is most often employees, as discussed elsewhere in this book, who were verbally or physically abused when they made mistakes as a child. To ask them to improve upon work they have done implies they have failed in some way—or they should have done it right the first time—and if they had, there would be no need for the improvement.

If you have such a person in your organization, as a member of your family, or within your close circle of friends, your task is daunting, yet doable.

First, it is important to establish your organization or home as a place where mistakes are acceptable. You must sing this song often, as you are attempting to overcome years of programming by teachers, family, or friends who taught that mistakes were wrong, and that we don't talk about our mistakes, and if we do, it is whispered quietly, in hushed tones, behind closed doors, and not in front of other people.

Second, it is imprtant to sing the praises of continuous improvement. Always ask, "How can we improve upon this product or presentation?" Let's hold it up to a bright light and think about and discuss how we can make it better. Listen intently and with an open mind to the discussion, even if you were part of the team or the individual who put your heart and soul into creating the concept in the first place. Everything we do should evolve and change and continue to be made better. You must believe in that.

Alas, in many cases, those two combined messages will fall on deaf ears. Oftentimes, there is an individual who just does not get it; no matter what you say, she will look on your attempts to improve upon her work as her personal failure.

Here is how I approached an otherwise valuable coworker who had been "mistake abused" as a child and was super-sensitive to even a

> ### The Failure Factor
>
> Help others embrace failure. We're not alone in this world. Lending a helping hand goes without saying. We're not talking about suffering here; we're talking about learning. What actions might you take to compassionately support other people when they fail, help them carry on, and encourage them to achieve even greater failures— and successes?

hint that work she had recently completed for me could some-how be improved. I went to visit her in her office (most people prefer the familiar surroundings of their own space when the boss is about to initiate a warm and caring heart-to-heart conversation). I told her that I thought we had different ex-periences in our lives as we grew up.

I explained that, when I was in high school, I had a foot-ball coach who was one of my greatest teachers. He believed strongly in analyzing, dissecting, and discussing, in a very public way, our mistakes. The coach filmed our football games, and, the day after each game, the entire team would gather and watch the films. Our coach would run the film play by play, oftentimes frame by frame in slow motion, both forward and backward, telling us when we did a technique correctly, or when we did a technique incorrectly. It was an incredible learning experience to watch, on slow-motion film, and see that if you had taken one step in the opposite direc-tion you might have picked up an additional yard or two on the play, or perhaps broken free and ran for a touchdown. We did this so often that it became an experience we all came to enjoy and desire. The mistakes we made became cause for celebration, as the learning experience was so beneficial. Now we were empowered by the knowledge of how to do it right, and couldn't wait for the next game. One year our team went undefeated (the only time in a long athletic career in which perfection in the win-loss column was obtained).

I went on to tell my associate that I didn't believe she had that same experience when she was growing up. I ex-plained that I felt relaxed and comfortable and enjoyed con-tinually improving our work because my childhood experiences, particularly with my football coach, had made me keenly aware of the potential payoff. She confessed that she had quite the opposite experience growing up, as her parents were hard on her when she struggled with learning experiences, even to the point of calling her stupid, and that my way sounded far more desirable. Following our conver-sation, we never had another problem discussing how to improve the work, and we went on to work together for more than 20 years. She was unusual in her ability to quickly embrace change, as most are not able to change their perception of self-improvement that easily.

When appropriate, and with permission, it is beneficial to record new business presentations and analyze them in an attempt to discern what was done right or wrong, and how it can be done better next time. It has to be done in a caring and helpful way. You need to establish before you start that it takes intestinal fortitude to stand up in front of a roomful of total strangers with relatively minimal knowledge of their company, while they know it inside out, telling them how you would help their company throughout the next five to 10 years. Establish that your people are heroes just for having the guts to step up to the plate. It's relatively easy to sit back in the comfort of a conference room chair with no pressure on you and dissect how we could have done a presentation better, which is precisely one of the many reasons why critiquing is so valuable. It is damn hard to be on the firing line in front of large groups and perform at a high level. After the fact, with the benefit of time and without pressure, you can gain great insights to improve your game and win future presentations more often. That is why analyzing, in a post-mortem environment, is so incredibly valuable. You would be foolish not to do it and benefit from the learning experience it provides. However, you have to cut those people on the firing line lots of slack, and in no way can the analysis be used to criticize them for not finding the right words or executing the perfect response. The only exception to that rule would be if they did not prepare properly for the presentation. But if they put their best effort forward and made mistakes, you have to congratulate them for the effort and for the courage to analyze it. Those are two admirable traits for which they should receive lavish praise, not ridicule for missteps.

Sadly, the people who refuse to try to improve upon their past efforts are condemned to live their lives in mediocrity. They will never obtain "the perfect season" because they are terrified of self-analysis with an eye toward trying to improve future performances. If they have a leadership role in your organization, they will not allow your organization to grow and improve because they are fearful of discussing their own shortcomings, rather than embracing their mistakes, learning how to correct them and moving on, stronger for having looked inside and celebrated their failures or repeated their successes.

Throughout the years, I have had confrontations with people in both my personal and business life over this issue. Not everyone shares my enthusiasm for self-analysis and self-improvement. Looking at my past efforts has been such a positive influence in my life that I have difficulty understanding when others don't embrace my experience. As George Santayana said, "Those who cannot remember the past are condemned to repeat it."

CHAPTER INSIGHTS
Each Step Takes You Closer to Success or Failure

- **Small celebrations.** Progress should be celebrated as a significant accomplishment. If you're shooting for a big goal, congratulate yourself and others on your team all along the way. Whether you ultimately succeed or fail, your accomplishments deserve recognition and praise.

- **Hold a post-mortem.** Critiquing your actions after a project is completed is a good way to improve results. It can be very motivating to a project team to know that even a less-than-ideal experience will not be repeated. Be sure to document the new procedures or game plans right away to get the most benefit from this process.

- **What could you do better?** Are there aspects of your own performance in which you accept less than you know you are capable of? With awareness and practice you can develop greater mastery and elevate areas of your life. The idea is not that one needs to be good at everything, but that one fulfills his or her potential.

18

Losing Control

*If things seem really under control, you're not
going fast enough.*
—Mario Andretti

I routinely go on long bike rides with a group of cyclists. It is interesting to watch the negotiations that take place when we meet and discuss the selection of that day's route. Generally there is a doctor or two who are on call and need to stay close to home and do the routine loops we always do. Next up there are a few cyclists whose spouses give them a hard time for leaving the house and enjoying themselves for more than an hour. They can't ride far from home. They generally form a coalition with the on-call doctors to stay close and do the same old loops again and again. And then there are others, like me, who are tired of the same old roads and will go to great lengths to explore unknown venues, requiring everyone to ride outside of their comfort zones and farther from home. There is something about riding or running in an area where you have never been before that expands the mind and awakens the senses. But all of the cyclists are struggling to obtain the same thing: control. In this case they are trying to control where they will spend the next two to three hours of their lives.

People are uncomfortable when they don't know how far they are traveling or when they will be home or which routes they will take. To surrender yourself to someone else's decision of where you will spend the next few hours of your life can be a relatively traumatic experience for many people.

When people give up control they can become irritated with the group leaders.

These control issues are evident in our work environments too. People want to know where the company is going, how it will get there, and what their roles will be in helping the company achieve its goals. That is why companies that set goals for both themselves and their employees are more successful, because goals provide a measure of control to all participants: "I get it: this is where the company is going and this is what I have to do to help it get there," they think. It takes away the fear of the unknown and provides a sense of control.

Control is such an important issue that it can have a negative impact on a person's health and well-being. A study published in *The Lancet*, a British medical journal, found that those with little control over their job responsibilities were at a 50-percent-higher risk of developing symptoms of coronary heart disease. The study explained that, when we lose control, our body produces elevated levels of fibrinogen, a protein that binds blood cells together to form clots, and increases the risk of heart attack. Giving our work teams or employees control over their own destiny can actually contribute to reducing the risk of heart attack and other stress-related illnesses. The human body is an incredible machine if we take proper care of it.

But health is just the tip of the iceberg. Accomplishing something great most often requires a leader to step up and lead the troops into battle, in the business sense. And there are invariably many different paths one can take to achieve success in battle. If we allow the people who work for us to have input and control over the path we take, we are far more likely to be successful. If I dictate the battle plan, it becomes *my* plan and those I work with have little or no control or ownership in the plan. On the other hand, if I can get the troops to see the general vision of where we want to go and what we should end up accomplishing, and then involve them in the planning so they have control, the chances for success are greatly improved because they become stakeholders in the plan and share control of its successful execution.

Ad agencies are notorious for having unusual working hours and we tried to turn this to our favor by giving our associates control over their own destiny. Creating catalogs and Websites often takes periods of great effort followed by periods when little goes on. Most agencies have a traffic department that schedules all of the work and moves it through the company. We had no traffic department, and our schedules were a collaborative effort between creative and account management. Those involved discussed and agreed to the schedule before they began work so each department had ownership in the schedule and control over its establishment. For example, in the production cycle of a catalog or Website, everyone desires enough time to deliver his or her best effort to the process. Merchandisers wanted to scour the markets looking for the latest innovations, waiting until the last possible moment to select and manufacture their product. Our creative people wanted sufficient time to write copy, photograph products, and design layouts. Our color technicians wanted to make certain colors match so "what you see is what you get" and returns were kept at a minimum. Print production and electronic programmers wanted enough time to correctly execute everyone's work and mail the catalog or launch the Website to our clients' customers.

Deadlines were critical to our clients' success, as they generate needed cash for their business, so we treated deadlines with ultimate reverence. I know our people worked weekends and, in a handful of extreme cases, around the clock to meet deadlines, but most often they were able to follow a reasonable schedule and get the work done within normal working hours. If they ever did need to come in on a weekend it was their decision and not mine (or, worse yet, my direct order), as they had control over their own schedule. No surprises, and most importantly, no heart-damaging loss of control.

When we do gather for those long bike rides and the route negotiations begin, I play a mental game with myself by turning myself over to the group decision-making process and going willingly with whatever route the group decides. Stepping out of the negotiations gives me a great view

> **The Failure Factor**
>
> Share control. Responsibility and accountability increase when we have a say in the plan.

of the process. But much the way G. Gordon Liddy would sleep in trees to gain control over his fear of heights, I do it as a reminder to myself that not being in control is mildly uncomfortable, and as a leader I need to do my best to make certain I am giving as much control as possible to those I work with. Maintaining unreasonable control is an easy yet abusive thing to do when you are a leader. It gives those in control a false sense of power over others. In reality, the more power and control you give to others, the more power and control you retain, as those around you become loyal and comfortable with your thoughtful leadership. You could never convince an overly controlling leader of that, but it is a fact of business life.

CHAPTER INSIGHTS
Give It Up

- Do you lead with an iron fist or a velvet glove? Are there areas of your business or your life in which you find yourself exercising tight control? How would it feel to share control? Give up control? It can be a liberating exercise and exciting for all involved.
- How does excess control or lack of control show itself in your business? Your life?
- How does excess control or the lack of control influence your role as a leader or partner?
- Do you view control as a way to prevent failure?
- Does your control prevent people from getting things done efficiently?
- Does your excess control take responsibility away from others who share a stake in the outcome?

19

More Valuable Than Money

Leaders don't create followers,
they create more leaders.
—Tom Peters

Early in my career, I read a survey that said the number-one thing employees seek in their jobs is a chance to learn and grow. Learning and growing ranked ahead of money, health insurance, work environment, vacation time, profit sharing, and everything else you might have guessed. I remember as a young manager being surprised that money did not occupy the top spot. I was not only young, but also naïve. From a management standpoint it seemed too good to be true: The more opportunities we provided employees to learn and grow, the more satisfied they would become with their jobs, while at the same time becoming more loyal and more valuable to the company and our clients. Talk about a win-win situation!

The opportunity to learn and grow is also something I value highly for myself, and one of my greatest resources to achieve personal and business growth have been business books. Dollar for dollar, giving an associate a great business book is the best investment a business owner can make. I can't get the checkbook out fast enough when someone shows an interest in a book. Books are filled with stories from people who have tried and failed, and perhaps triumphed in the end, and they are all willing to share their experiences with your coworkers for the nominal cost of the book, so as to get the benefit without living the failure. Talk about celebrating failure! Books provide a limitless opportunity to learn about success and failure from others' experiences.

123

From time to time, when a book significantly impacted the culture at Ovation, we brought the author to La Crosse, Wisconsin, to spend a day with us. Tom Peters was our first visiting author. We immersed ourselves in his zealous, personal service philosophy that resonated years beyond his visit.

Joyce Wycoff, the author of *Mindmapping: Your Personal Guide to Exploring Creativity and Problem-Solving*, came and demonstrated her unique style of big-picture, undisciplined note-taking, which I still use today.

Ed Burnett, Joan Throckmorton, and Katie Muldoon were other authors with specialized advertising expertise who shared their time and wisdom with us.

> ### The Failure Factor
>
> Learn from others. If others have tried and failed—and learned to succeed—understand the lessons they have to teach. It may not be as memorable as living through the failure yourself, but it isn't as painful or expensive either.

James Autry, author of my all-time favorite business book, *Love and Profit*, visited us as the result of a collaborative session with the local public school district. It started with a robust discussion I had with my daughter's school superintendent about one of the school's policies and its unwillingness to change. I sent a copy of *Love and Profit* to the superintendent and told him his school district needed to read the book and adapt and change. He called me up, laughing, and told me that he had also sent James Autry's book to maybe a half-dozen people throughout the years along with a letter much like mine. It turns out, James Autry was his favorite business author as well. It opened the door to a beautiful friendship that brought James Autry to La Crosse. It redefined the term *strange bedfellows* when a school district and an advertising agency worked together in this way. It's a great example of how a partnership with another business or an organization within your community can help defray the costs associated with bringing an author to your place of business.

We bought everyone in the company a copy of best-selling author Jeff Thull's book, *Mastering the Complex Sale*. People started quoting the book around the office as though it was the Bible. The book's insights permeated our organization, completely changing the way we approached selling our services. We again made the educational investment and brought in the author to work with us and help us better understand the book. The author's presence and knowledge accelerated the learning process in the company. It is exciting to engage an author with a fresh perspective in a discussion about your business challenges. Giving employees the opportunity to study directly with a respected author, with a book on the best-selling charts, helps them learn and grow in an intense, unique way and sends the message that the company wants to invest in their personal and career development.

CHAPTER INSIGHTS
The Lessons We Learn From Others

- **Read a good book lately?** I've read many books throughout the years that so impressed me that I immediately purchased copies for all my associates. I consider it a small investment to make in a corporate culture. I used to do it more frequently, but now that more of everyone's time has shifted to reading online, I find myself forwarding e-newsletters, white papers, and other interesting content to my peers and associates.
- **Spend time online and on the front lines.** Everyone knows the Internet is a great resource for finding information, from fact-based official sites to opinion blogs. You can save time and resources using the Internet to find valuable case studies, customer comments, corporate information, and other research. It's also a great way to tap into various cultures, customer segments,

and industries when you research a market to gain a better understanding of current, relevant issues.

- **Cross-training, anyone?** Learning a new business skill or way of thinking doesn't always have to come from an outside expert. Giving your people the chance to learn other internal jobs can improve flexibility, increase job satisfaction, and enhance longevity with your organization. Teaching what it is you do to your associates improves your understanding of your own job. Learning what others do can give associates a greater understanding and appreciation of each individual's contribution to the organization.

Those who are ready for a new challenge and like what they learn about other jobs within your organization can perhaps change careers within your company, rather than leave for an outside company.

20

Investing in People: The HR ROI

If you want to build a ship, don't drum up people to collect wood and don't assign them tasks and work, but rather teach them to long for the sea.
—Antoine de Saint-Exupery

I am always amazed at how learning and teaching opportunities present themselves to us, often in the most ordinary aspects of our lives. One of the most fruitful seems to be with the "burning questions" that people often find the hardest to ask of our leaders. Encouraging associates to ask questions can uncover a gold mine of misunderstood leadership positions that can be discussed and better understood by all.

An associate once asked me why I would spend money to bring in a consultant instead of putting the money toward deserving staff salaries, of which I am certain he considered himself a part. In this particular case, the incoming consultant was Toni Louw, who assists companies in polishing their presentation skills. Toni is one of the leading authorities in the country on how to sell creative. It is a joy to watch him work his magic. My associate thought that his own value was somehow diminished because I felt the need to spend money on a consultant to further develop his skills.

Nothing could be further from the truth. Spending decisions should never be made in terms of money spent versus another person's salary. Certainly as a businessperson, in the back of my mind (*way* in the back), when we commit money to something, we are aware that the $15,000 we spend on a consultant will not be available for salaries—mine included—or any other expense for that matter. But that fact is not much more than a blip on the radar screen when deciding to make an investment in equipment, training, or people.

Here is a more revealing decision thought process: If we invest this $15,000 in a consultant's expertise, will he help raise the professional skill level and performance of associates enough to make a significant financial contribution to the bottom line? Will this investment in training and education pay off and make money? The next account win might be because of some extra tip or direction a consultant gave us in that $15,000 training session. If he makes the small margin of difference in winning a million-dollar account that stays for three years, then that $15,000 training seminar was an excellent investment.

> ## The Failure Factor
> Release the stress of failure. Give your body a physical outlet and the mental stress will flow out. Approach failure as an exercise that trains you to succeed. You may not finish a marathon as fast as you had hoped the first time you try. However, in time, with the training and the wisdom, the strength and the experience you gain from failing, you will finish successfully.

Or perhaps a consultant will raise the level of how well our work is presented so that a client decides to sign a long-term contract. Or one of our clients says, after a particularly great presentation, "You know, we were going to give a second new project to a different company, but now we are giving it to you because you made such an excellent case for your company." Then the $15,000 investment in coaching was worth it.

When, for $15,000, you can greatly improve the way people perform their jobs, then it only takes a small overall improvement on everyone's part to make the investment pay off in a huge way. If we greatly improve how we communicate with clients or keep a single client for an extra year, then it's worth the investment.

There is another added value to the investment in education that can't be overlooked. After completing this education, the individuals become more valuable to the company, and they increase their potential for their entire career as well. They gain the skills to be more successful, and no doubt will earn more money throughout their lifetimes, whether they continued working for me or moved on to another opportunity. This kind of investment in people should mean a great deal to an individual when he or she chooses a place to work.

I apply this same mental process with most purchases; exercise equipment is another excellent example. If just one more person starts working out on a consistent basis because of the addition of a $2,000 Stairmaster he or she becomes attached to, and that person is healthier, avoids illness, and misses less work, there is a payback. The person also, by exercising and staying healthy, won't spread illness to others at work.

CHAPTER INSIGHTS
Always Calculate the Payback

- **What's the ROI?** We routinely gave clients at Ovation a detailed return on their investment for the work we performed. An ROI sets off a chain reaction of positive events. If I give your company a proposal on what it will cost for us to build a database of your best customers and engage them in an ongoing dialogue about how your company's products or services solve their problems, it requires me to have a thorough understanding of how you go to market and how my actions will benefit your company and when you will realize a profit from my actions. Otherwise, why on earth would you consider my proposal?

It is similar for our family, friends, and co-workers when we make investments in their personal growth and education. Investing in associates' professional growth and health just makes good business sense. It's not only the right thing to do, but is also most often a breathtakingly brilliant investment in their future that will pay off for both parties many times over. We know it, but do they always know it? Not by the question I was asked about consultant salaries at the beginning of this chapter. The employee is silently thinking, "There he goes again, off on some tangent spending our hard-earned money when he could be giving me that money in the form of a salary increase."

The lesson that I wanted my associates to take away from the decision to hire the consultant is that we invested in their education *because* they were so valuable and *because* we wanted them to continue on that path. A good, open-book company will share the thinking behind the ROI numbers with its clients and its employees.

I enjoy being asked tough questions by people I work with because they are the very questions that are the most important to answer. Encourage and then answer the tough questions, and good things will happen to your company and its workforce.

21

Let Me Help You Find a New Job

*It takes courage to show your
dreams to someone else.*

—Erma Bombeck

Throughout the course of my agency's 31-year history, it benefitted from a low turnover rate. I believe one of the major contributing factors was our philosophy of honest communications, even to the point of helping associates find a new job if theirs was simply not right for them or if they wanted to pursue another opportunity.

To better explain our philosophy, I'd like to share a passage from the agency's personnel manual with you:

"If you desire to leave Ovation for a new job, for any reason (an advancement, higher pay, new location, new challenge, burnout, boredom, or whatever), please feel free to speak with your manager, human resources, or come directly to me. We will help you, can help you, and have helped many associates. If you wish to leave, I promise you I will use all of my powers of persuasion and any contacts or influence to assist you. I understand some feel our views on this subject are unusual, but you've probably known we are not your typical company since we first met."

In one instance, an associate wanted to work in an area that we could not offer. Providing a job reference for him during his search made an outstanding impression on the new company's human resources department. It also demonstrated to the new company that this was an above-board, open, and honest person who had such a great relationship with his current employers that, when he told them he was looking for a different career, they wanted him to succeed to the extent that they helped him in the search and gave him a stunning job recommendation. (I confess, it made a great statement about Ovation, too.) The associate got his new job. We also counseled him on our generous, yet complex, profit sharing, ESOP (employee stock ownership plan), performance bonus plan, and what a comparable salary would be at a company that paid a straight salary without these benefits.

Another example similar to this one of another Ovation associate who chose the open dialogue route to a job change is Paul, one of our vice presidents, who learned of a job opportunity he had looked upon as a dream job as a young man. I used all of my sales skills to help convince his prospective new employer that Paul was an outstanding candidate. Paul had been loyal to Ovation for 14 years; of course I would return the favor. Again, it made an extremely strong statement to the prospective employer about Paul's character and his open and honest relationship with me. All candidates being equal, which one would you rather hire: the typical candidate who says, "God, whatever you do, don't tell my current employer I'm interviewing," or the one with an open relationship with his boss, and whose boss raves about him or her? It just gives the potential employer one more opportunity to judge the character of the candidate. And when you only spend a few hours interviewing with a prospective employee, you are looking for any clue or help you can get about that individual's character.

> **The Failure Factor**
>
> Embrace change. Failure and change often come together. If you fall down, be open to the opportnities to change yourself or your environment. Accept a helping hand when it is offered. Offer one where it is needed.

Paul ultimately got the job offer, but turned it down. And he remained a valuable associate for seven more years before eventually moving on to a new position. His desire to consider other job opportunities did not negatively affect his position at Ovation, and that is the way it should be. The idea is to create a place so unique that people want to stay. And if you give people the freedom to leave, even offer to help them leave if they so choose and thus give them the control, they are actually far more apt to stay.

I, and all of my associates, worked hard to make Ovation a great place to work, but I would have to be extremely naive to think that, from time to time, someone isn't going to get a better job offer or feel like leaving, for any number of good reasons. Openly discussing these opportunities can most often strengthen your relationship with the right employer. If there is something about your job that you don't like, rather than lose you to another company (after all the time, energy, and training invested in you), forward-thinking companies can restructure your current job or move you to another department. Sometimes that's possible and sometimes it's just not, but at least it can be discussed and considered. We were able to do it for many employees, including me. Even the president can get tired of the same job! Especially after 30 years. I reinvented my position at Ovation many times. People sometimes need to change and grow, and I am not only a firm believer in that theory, but an example of it.

A good company owes you this kind of effort and loyalty, in exchange for your effort and your loyalty. An open dialogue gives you the opportunity to address problems you might be having at work, if your reasons for leaving are things that can be changed.

Another reason for my offer to assist associates in finding a new job is that, in some cases, an employee may be unhappy in his or her job, for whatever reason. I don't want people working for my company if they would be happier somewhere else. That is a no-win situation for both parties, and for all associates who would have to work alongside an unhappy person. I cheerfully helped associates move on to other opportunities if they were unhappy. I have resigned myself to the fact that, as hard as I might try—and I try very hard—there are too many opposing forces to keep everyone 100 percent happy, year in and year out. Sometimes it's just time to move on. (See Chapter 30 for more about moving on.)

There is one final reason you should tell your boss that you're looking for a new job, before you look: The world is a small place, getting smaller every day, and most of the people in it are bad actors and terrible at keeping secrets. In the majority of cases, your employer will know or hear about your job hunt anyway. Almost immediately! I can count on one hand, with several fingers to spare, the number of times I was surprised by someone's resignation in the past 30 years. One of our associates from Florida's "Gator Nation" had his office walls covered with blue and orange Gator sports decor. Every Friday during football season he wore the Florida uniform to work and looked mildly depressed when there wouldn't be coverage on local television, which was most often. If you've ever met anyone from Gainesville, Florida, you know what I'm talking about.

"No kidding, Lee. You want to move back to Florida to be near your beloved Gators? Wow, I never had a clue!"

I am aware that some of you will read this and still not be able to discuss a possible career change with your boss. Or you may be a boss who simply cannot take the time for this effort. I also understand that, sadly, not all bosses are open to discussing such alternatives. I suppose it goes against much of what we think we know about people. People often think the boss will explode, and at some companies the boss does explode. If you think about it, my position on this subject only makes good business sense. And good business sense should drive our decisions.

Whenever my associates left, I was always the first person to rise from my chair, walk around my desk, congratulate them, shake their hands, and wish them the very best of luck. Sometimes I even gave them a big hug.

CHAPTER INSIGHTS
Use Me As a Reference

- **What goes up must come down.** Just in case you need another reason to be generous with your time or support, remember the old adage, "We meet the same people on our way up the career ladder as on the way down." That may not be true for everyone, but in thinking about how our work lives are extending into our later years, it may be more probable in the future.

- **It's not what you know; it's who you know.** Contacts and networks are more important now in our social society. You never know who you may meet on the other end of the phone line or conference table at your next client appointment. Wouldn't it be nice to have it be a friendly, happy encounter?

- **Karma, the Golden Rule, or whatever moral compass you follow.** Doing nice things for other people; doing the right thing; being generous; or just helping someone. Nothing makes me feel better or happier.

22

Negative Listening

*If you have made mistakes, there is always
another chance for you. You may have a fresh
start any moment you choose, for this thing we
call "failure" is not the falling down, but the
staying down.*
—Mary Pickford

A company says a lot about itself through the first impression its people make when they greet and listen to their customers.

I was recently searching for a facility to accommodate an upcoming meeting. As I walked into a prospective local venue, there did not seem to be anyone around to help me. I finally noticed that in the corner of this large meeting room was a customer service rep who appeared to be in charge. She had her head down and was typing away at a keyboard. I waited a few minutes and, when she did not look up or come to me, I walked over to her. I said that I was interested in renting this meeting space and would like to take a quick tour to see if it would meet our needs.

"When would you be interested in renting it?" she asked. "We're really busy this time of year."

"Well, probably in the next two or three weeks," I replied, and added, "We just need it for two or three hours in the morning, probably from 8 a.m. to 11 a.m."

She retorted, "Well, nobody is here until 9 a.m. so that would be a problem. Did you say you needed it on Monday?"

"No, I didn't say which day we needed it; we haven't picked a day yet."

"Oh, because we're closed on Mondays," she said. The woman was so negative that it actually affected her hearing. Filtering words through negative perceptions can affect what we hear. There was no way this woman wanted to come in on her off day, and it affected and distorted the way she listened and the things she heard. She was eager to have opportunities to say no.

> ## The Failure Factor
>
> Set an example by being positive. Even when a failure occurs or an outcome seems less than ideal, look for the positive elements within it and encourage others to do the same.

After her negative pitch, I took a quick tour of the room anyway, and it fell short of what I was looking for. I am certain the company representative and her negative service adversely impacted my perception of the facility.

Although I went on to find a suitable meeting room elsewhere, I continued to think about how we listen and how a leader might reshape that customer service experience.

The customer service rep could have begun by acknowledging my presence and coming over to greet me. She should not have told me how busy they were. The customer never wants to hear about your problems. It's not about us; it's about them. They have enough problems of their own. They want you to solve their problems.

She could have then said, "Sir, our room is available Tuesday through Friday, but if you absolutely need it on Monday, we'll make special arrangements to have someone here. The room is available from 9:00 in the morning until 5:00 in the afternoon, but if you need to start at 8:00, I will arrange to have someone here and make sure the room is open and ready."

I wonder how the facility would have looked to me after receiving such a positive and welcoming greeting.

When I say I encourage mistakes as a path to success, this is NOT the kind of mistake I mean. In fact, quite the opposite. Employees must look for an opportunity to say yes to the customer and to present information in a positive way. Better to make a mistake being positive than create a negative impression. And if you don't know the answer to a question, better to say, "That's a good question! I don't have that information right now, but I'll find the answer and get back to you."

This customer service rep is not alone in her use of negative listening perceptions. A great example of this happened to radio talk show host Don Imus. After his highly publicized firing for having made an extremely inappropriate comment on the air about a women's basketball team, he returned to radio and television a year later. He had been so vilified by the publicity from the event that people who watched his new TV program called the station to complain they heard Imus using the "F" word on the air, which he of course had not done. He had been painted so badly by the press that it affected how people listened and what they heard. But in fact, Imus is probably the quintessential example of celebrating failure, as he studied what he had done wrong, learned from his failure, and came back stronger than ever with a far more racially balanced and superior program.

If, for example, we perceive that one of our coworkers is hopelessly not making progress in a certain area where we have been coaching him to improve, we need to make certain we listen with an open and positive mind or we will miss opportunities to "hear" attempts at improvement. If we have clients that said no to ideas we presented many times in the past, we need to listen harder for their attempts at change or we will put them in a box and miss it. The idea is to improve the way we listen so we don't become like a certain customer service rep that was so overly fixated on not working on a Monday that all she could hear was Monday.

CHAPTER INSIGHTS
Everything Matters

- **You never get a second chance to make a good impression.** When guests are visiting your company, make certain everyone in the company has been provided with their name, along with the correct pronunciation, title, and anything else that would be helpful. Encourage associates who encounter the VIP guests, even by chance—or especially by chance—to stop and introduce themselves and thank them for coming to your company. Openly greeting office visitors makes an incredible impression.

- **Post a welcome message with names in the reception area.** Do something special if it is a new client or first-time visitor. Our agency had a wall where we hung the logos of any company for which we worked. The first time a new company visited, after becoming a client, we placed its logo on the wall in the reps' presence and said a few nice words welcoming them to Ovation.

  So many companies do so little to stand out; you must differentiate yourself in the most positive way possible. The other interesting thing about our wall of logos was the care it demanded. We put our clients' logos on a foam board material and then attached the board to the wall with sticky temporary glue that doesn't leave a mark or a hole in the wall. But invariably each logo would eventually fall off the wall, and our associates had to stop and pick up the piece of foam board and press it back up. It served as a metaphor for life: Those logos needed constant attention and handling to remain valuable clients.

23

Even Geniuses Can Fail

Try as hard as we may for perfection, the net result of our labors is an amazing variety of imperfectness. We are surprised at our own versatility in being able to fail in so many different ways.
—Samuel McChord Crothers

I once worked with a business associate who was a member of Mensa, the association for people with genius-level IQs, and she was not bashful about name-dropping her membership in that prestigious organization to her coworkers. I will return to her in a moment.

Listening is an important skill I test for during an interview process. I will stop talking in midsentence, as though I am lost in deep thought, and I'll wait to see if the person being interviewed is disciplined enough to remain silent and listen carefully for the next key statement to potentially connect with me and eventually land a job, or if he or she will become nervous with the dead air and feel compelled to fill it with noise. If interviewees don't listen to me, I assume they won't listen to a client or customer, and it is impossible to solve the customer's problem if you don't hear it. A service business, similar to an advertising agency and many other businesses, requires the handling of thousands of detailed bits of information. A client may convey a desire for a change in the way we positioned its brand, or want something as mundane as a change in price or the color of a product. And, as was the case with our Mensa star, if you fail to listen to the client and correctly capture the new information being communicated, then you appear incompetent, as does your company.

I once gave our Mensa lady changes and new directives on a project we were working on and I noticed that the requested changes were not always being made. So one day as I was giving her some specific client changes, I noticed that, while she was listening to me, she was failing to capture any of my comments on paper.

I finally asked her, "How are you remembering all of these details I'm directing you to act on?"

She shrugged and said, "I'm a member of Mensa, and I remember everything."

I then gently reminded her of several items I had asked her to execute things that had gone undone. She was smart enough to recognize that I had made a good point, and she made the rapid conversion to taking notes and using a to-do list. The problem went away quickly.

> **The Failure Factor**
>
> Fail smarter. Failure does not equate to a lack of intelligence. People of all intellects and skill levels fail. Be willing to learn from it and fail smarter next time.

It does not matter how smart you are. No one can remember every detail in an environment where you are surrounded by hundreds of rapidly changing details—which describes most businesses today. Yet, a to-do list receives little or no respect in our society. Comedians tell jokes about wives who make out a "honey-do list" for their husbands. Some people incorrectly think that when they were in high school or college they were smart enough to remember all of their assignments, so why should that change now that they are in the business world? Of course, in college you slept until 10 in the morning and you only had four classes with maybe two major assignments per semester. Now you're juggling 20 assignments at any given time, each containing hundreds of detailed items. The fact is, the sheer number of details that come at you in a business environment are astronomical compared with our experiences in college.

A to-do list committed to paper is liberating, allowing the mind to relax and be creative and solve challenges in any order it chooses. Perplexing challenges can wait until the idea has had time to be fully contemplated. You may glance at it from time to time, aware that the problem must be solved. You may choose to give the item some occasional attention, or you may choose to turn away from it until you are in the creative zone and the solutions start to flow from your mind.

It does not take genius-level intelligence, or membership in Mensa, to recognize that you will accomplish more if you keep track of your challenges and assignments in some kind of "to-do list." Successful accomplishments certainly have the effect of making you look smart.

CHAPTER INSIGHTS
Learn Something From Your Triumphs and Failures

- **Establish goals and keep a to-do list.** Some experts have estimated that committing goals to paper (or your hard drive) increases your chances of accomplishing the goal by 40 percent. Writing your goals down makes you more accountable and gives you a clearer target at which to aim.

- **Keep a "Puff" file of your successes.** When I first entered the business world, someone told me to keep a "Puff" file—in other words, to retain every positive communiqué I received in life and put it in a file. Awards, accolades, and personal thank-you notes all went into a file marked "Puff." The concept behind a Puff file is that on some rainy day, when life is crushing your every attempt to survive, you read this file of wonderful accomplishments and you instantly feel better about yourself. When the

Internet came along, I did an electronic version of the Puff file. I must have really admired the person who gave me the advice, as I am generally not good at keeping historical records of events, yet I dutifully followed this one. I am glad I did, as it serves as a historical record of my accomplishments, even though, to date, I haven't really studied it.

- **Keep a file marked "Celebrating Failure."** When I decided to write a book and capitalize on failures and successes, I started another file attempting to capture all of the lessons learned in the trenches. So I am keeping two files that are almost at opposite ends of the learning spectrum. I can go to one file and read about accomplishments, or I can go to the other file and be reminded of every bad decision I have made in the last 30 years and what I learned from it. I confess, the Puff file almost instantly bores me, and I have never been able to get past four or five of the latest entries before I wander off and do something else. (I have the attention span of a small cat on a good day.) On the other hand, I am riveted by the stories in the Celebrating Failure file. I am more proud for having stepped up in the attempt to succeed than I am in my accomplishments (yawn). I'm sure some day I will come to appreciate the positive contributions, especially the personal notes from those I admire. But if you want to learn, grow, and improve, keep your vision on celebrating failure, as that is where you will learn to conquer the future.

24

Keep Your Edge

*Any activity becomes creative when the doer cares
about doing it right, or doing it better.*
—John Updike

I originally started work in the advertising agency business
as a copywriter, and subsequently became active in presenting TV and radio creative. One of the things I really
enjoyed about my job was presenting concepts to clients and
to fellow associates. What I enjoyed the most about presenting concepts was the challenge of selling people on my creative ideas. It was also interesting to see how creative ideas
and concepts would then evolve after more and more people
started putting their fingerprints on the original seed of the
idea.

As our advertising agency grew, my role in creative
changed drastically—to the point at which my new job became primarily one of managing the company and the growing group of people working with me. This change in role is
a common occurrence among entrepreneurs. Entrepreneurs
have a certain skill set, such as creating advertising, but as
the company grows and changes, they end up managing the
business and doing less and less of the creative work that
made them successful in the beginning—the reason why they
started the company in the first place. It certainly kept things
interesting to constantly reinvent my role, and it is probably
why I stayed with the same company for more than 30 years.

Occasionally, the opportunity presented itself to jump
back to my old creative role, as happened when an old friend
of mine from college, John Swendrowski, president of

Northland Cranberries, came to us with a challenge. His company was struggling to avoid declaring Chapter 11 bankruptcy. Initially, Northland wanted us to do some public relations for them, and later some advertising. We had handled a few packaged goods advertising accounts in the past, but our experience was not as deep as it was in other markets, so I wanted to be involved and make sure we were doing everything right. John was an old friend so I went along with the team to the creative pitch when we first won the business. It was a great opportunity to get back to my roots.

Energized by this new challenge, I picked up paper and pencil and started writing commercial copy and doing storyboards just like I did when I was the one-man creative department. I enjoyed it immensely. I especially enjoyed presenting my creative concepts to the account team and then to the client. The team members had been pitching ideas to me for the past 10 years on most of our accounts. I often sat in and reviewed our presentations and attempted to improve them by offering plenty of comments. Now the shoe was on the other foot.

It was only a 30-second commercial. Suddenly, I was in a room with five people who are analyzing every nuance and every word in my ad. Some of them understood exactly what I was saying, whereas others were confused by the way I presented it. I thought most of the comments that day were excellent and insightful.

I then realized that, as the president of the company, I made many quick, day-to-day decisions in which no one gave me any input. On most days, I was a rapid-fire, unchecked decision-maker. For example, I once wrote a long letter to a brand-new client's reps attempting to convince them that we could continue to handle their national brand as well as an extremely small regional brand, located in our hometown, in the same product category. The letter was a two-page impassioned plea to allow us to keep working on both of the accounts. I sent the letter to our client without anyone's input—I certainly did not have to present the letter to five people and have them critique my every word. In some ways, when you become president and make a lot of decisions, you miss that; you miss that input and having others analyze your work and give you feedback as you do when you are part of a creative team.

After presenting my creative concepts to the team that day, I found myself going back and thinking about that letter and the multitude of daily decisions I made on my own. I cannot say I will always seek team input; that would be inefficient because there are an overwhelming number of decisions that a company president must make on a daily basis, yet since that day, I have attempted to seek more input. It was invigorating. It improved the results. It let me exercise some creative muscle, which felt great! It also motivated the team to have the shoe on the other foot and critique my work for a change. Never miss an opportunity to get in the trenches with the troops.

> ## The Failure Factor
>
> Constructive criticism helps you fail smarter. Invite critical input and feedback. Show that you can take it as well as dish it from those around you—your family, friends, colleagues, coworkers, and clients.

And as for my letter requesting permission from our new client to let us handle their national brand *and* our small regional brand client, they politely replied no. They demanded our exclusive attention, which I completely understood. The new national brand was going to be spending far more money, so we took our cue from the infamous informant, Deep Throat, in the book/movie *All the President's Men*, and followed the money.

CHAPTER INSIGHTS
Get Into the Trenches With the Troops

- **Don't lose touch.** One of the intangibles that contributed to my modest success as a business leader was my start as a one-man band. I did every job at the company and appreciated the time and talent it took to do each job. I have been the receptionist and the strategic planner. I have stuffed envelopes, and perhaps realized sooner than most that oftentimes it is better to hire outside suppliers to do tedious, repetitive work. Sit down next to Web developers and feel some compassion for what it takes for them to do their jobs. Anyone who thinks he or she is too busy to gain such understanding and compassion is sadly mistaken.

- **Keep your skills sharp.** It's difficult to lead without the respect of your team. Keeping your skills honed shows that you still know your stuff. You don't have to be perfect every time; it's not your job anymore to be Mr. Know-All-the-Details. Who better to teach than the one with the most experience?
- **Take it as well as you dish it.** Accepting criticism, even constructive criticism, can be hard. Show your team that you can take it as well as give it. Even if you don't agree with a comment, suspend your resistance and open yourself to a different point of view. Respond with a simple "Thank you" or "That's interesting," and make notes to consider the thoughts later.

25

Confronting Fear and Surviving the Epic Crisis

Cowards die many times before their deaths. The valiant never taste of death but once.

—William Shakespeare

Bad *news* and *good news* can be relative terms that people define differently based on how they "SEA" the world (through sex, education, and age). The number of business failures in this country, which is bad news, is staggering. Some sources report that four out of five business start-ups do not survive—and that is in a good economy. As a company continues to endure, its chances of survival improve with each passing year. But all companies during their lifetime have one or more "Come to Jesus" moments when their very existence on Earth is threatened. A few will survive the crisis, but, according to the statistics, most fail. Some business experts predict that many of our iconic brands may not survive the current economic turmoil. If it can happen to them, it can happen to you and me, and chances are that every business, even after it has survived the initial start-up phase, will still come up against a major crisis, or several, that will threaten its existence or present some engaging leadership challenges.

Leaders should view harbingers of potential crisis events in terms of leading and lagging indicators. The ad agency business is a particularly precarious business, because it is not uncommon for a single client, even when you are doing everything right, to represent 5 to 25 percent of your gross income, and there are many reports of agencies going as high as having 75 percent of their business from one client. But ad agencies don't have that market cornered. Most businesses in this country sadly fall within the 80/20 rule, in that 80 percent of their income is being generated by only 20 percent of their customers or clients. So when a client(s) leaves, representing a major portion of your business, it takes a skillful leader to survive such a crisis.

A leading indicator of impending crisis is a decline in the particular business sector in which your company specializes, thus beginning the slow erosion of that profit center, which might bring down your fragile empire. For example, in the 1980s my agency specialized in creating catalogs. You build one well and people tend to come to your door asking if you can build one for them. In the early 1980s, to purchase a single desktop computer equipped to produce catalogs cost $40,000. It was not economically feasible for small to mid-sized companies to purchase two or three desktop computers for their needs only, so they tended to hire an agency such as ours that could spread the high cost over many catalog companies. By 1988, the price of a desktop computer was down to $2,000—so low that most small to mid-sized companies could afford to purchase several and were more likely to produce their own catalogs inhouse (funny how they forget they need to hire, train, and manage a staff of top professionals to operate the computer, but that is another story). I cringed whenever I saw an ad for an Apple computer in the late 1980s (even though I was buying them like popcorn). The price of computers was a leading indicator we read early and moved quickly to diversify our creative offerings so as not to rely on catalog production for our income. You can do a great job of avoiding crisis if you do a great job reading early leading indicators.

On the other hand, a lagging indicator would be the actual firing or loss of a major piece of business that can quickly decimate your income and topple the empire you are working hard to create. Leading indicators occur early, and you have time to make adjustments. Lagging indicators occur later, most often too late to make adjustments in direction.

Terms that often get tossed around at the start of a major crisis, when good leaders are always listening intently and watching for leading and lagging indicators, are the old reliable terms *good news* and *bad news*. We had some bad news (in other words, our first major crisis) at Ovation in 1992 when our then-largest client, The Company Store, called at 3:30 p.m. on a Friday afternoon to tell me they had decided to declare bankruptcy. Being a student of leading indicators, I was painfully aware that perhaps the call was coming. But that didn't help to alleviate the gut-wrenching pain.

The Company Store had been battling with the banks, asking them to forgive part of a $50 million debt—affectionately referred to in the business as "take a haircut." If the lenders would forgive part of the debt (that is, the haircut), the monthly loan payments would be lowered and become more manageable, and the company felt it could survive and continue to pay the secured bank lenders and the unsecured creditors (that would be the poor, working-class suppliers such as Ovation), who had absolutely no say or power in the negotiations. An unsecured creditor has as much clout as a homeless person in a bank. Without a reduction in debt, The Company Store would declare bankruptcy and the secured lenders (the banks and insurance companies) would own the assets of the company that were secured with the loan agreement, and the unsecured creditors would be SOL. I did attend a meeting of unsecured creditors, and quickly calculated that the time I was losing attending the meeting was going to be more valuable than the amount of money I would ever recover. I also felt as though I was in a room with a bunch of losers, which in fact I was, and my $200,000 debt was among the highest in the unsecured category, which of course meant I was the biggest loser in the room! The banks and insurance companies were at the party for $50 million (secured losers). I thought about not attending the meetings, but I wanted to take in the entire failure experience as I felt it would serve as a personal, painful reminder not to put my company in this position a second time. I was also getting an education in high finance and learning new terms like *take a haircut*, which I hoped would make me popular at cocktail parties.

In the best-case scenario, a bankruptcy judge might disperse the assets and an unsecured creditor such as ourselves would end up being paid maybe 10 cents on the dollar. The Company Store was spending about $100,000 a month with us ($1.2 million a year), and owed us for two months of work, or $200,000. So $200,000 would, best case, in maybe a year, become $20,000. Frankly, I wasn't holding out much hope of that happening. Having a client declare bankruptcy is a double whammy, as not only do you lose the $200,000 they owe you, but they are no longer spending $100,000 a month with your company.

Managing Ovation out of that financial crisis didn't start on that Friday afternoon after the dreaded phone call that is permanently etched in my brain; it started years before, when we observed our client was taking on enormous debt and we felt they represented too large a part of our overall income. A potential crisis requires leaders to open their eyes to what is happening around them even though the desire is to relax, celebrate the current prosperity, and keep thinking happy thoughts about how brilliant you have recently become.

Anticipating crisis requires a disturbingly negative vigilance to the possibility of catastrophe occurring to your favorite account, which is not an easy or fun thing to do. The main emphasis of our plan was to "neutralize the gorilla." (A gorilla is an account or category of accounts that represents too large a share of your business.)

You don't want a gorilla account for many reasons, of which the potential of bankruptcy is only one. Here's why. Giving strategic advertising counsel to clients requires brutal honesty, which on occasion can piss off a client, who can retaliate by firing you. It is far easier to be brutally honest when a client's exit from your roster only causes a ripple of discomfort. This means there are two ways to neutralize the gorilla: either by taking on additional new clients, or by doing less business with the gorilla. I have always embraced the first option and rejected the second. I understand the risk with the second; it's just that we've always believed we should never give our competition a chance to get their foot in the door, and reducing a client's spending carries that risk. Or, stated a more ruthless way, "never give another agency your scraps." Thus we decided the cornerstone of managing our way out of what was perhaps on the radar as a potential crisis, was to take on new clients and neutralize the size of the gorilla.

Taking on new clients takes time and planning, which is why the early warning provided by the leading indicators becomes so important to managing crisis survival. If you have a million-dollar account that represents 10 percent of your business and you get a new million-dollar account in a new and diverse category, the gorilla has been reduced in size. You have established a beachhead in a new category that you can more easily build upon, until that new category becomes the new gorilla and the process starts all over again.

The 15-year saga of The Company Store and Ovation Marketing's relationship (see Chapter 5) did have its own unique denouement. The investment group that purchased the business from Terry Gillette, and years later declared bankruptcy, decided they had more fertile ground with their other business opportunities and sold The Company Store to one of its catalog competitors. The new owners were headquartered in New Jersey. The local hometown advantage we held with the company located in La Crosse was gone, and we did not survive the second change in ownership. However, I am happy to report that the company continues today (www.thecompanystore.com) and markets itself in much the same way we created for it back in the 1980s. It is a good feeling to know you were a part of helping to build something that has endured for 25-plus years.

An entrepreneur's number-one goal is to create something that lasts after he or she is gone. With that as our measure, both companies have been successful. Ovation's strategy to neutralize the gorilla worked to near perfection, as the absence of The Company Store income at the time of its departure was at a manageable level. The year it left, Ovation was able to pay the maximum amount allowed by law into our profit-sharing plan and our associates enjoyed above-average performance bonuses. It was an exciting time in both companies' histories.

Reflecting on the experience through the benefit of time brings back great memories, and even the "we've decided to declare bankruptcy" phone call seems mildly entertaining to me today. During The Company Store's glory days, to borrow a phrase from Bruce Springsteen, I often wondered what it would be like to no longer work on something you helped create, as the one certainty in agency/client relationships is that they all end. I am happy to report that life is good. After 15 years of describing "the natural warmth and comfort of luxurious European white down comforters," change is good. It was an incredible relationship and learning experience, and I use that knowledge nearly every day. Interestingly, about four years after The Company Store sale, we did participate in an agency shootout for the business with the New Jersey owners, but we did not win the account. Perhaps just as well, as I'm not sure I could have handled another 15 years of the same.

> ### The Failure Factor
>
> Neutralize the gorilla. Risk is a natural part of business, but how can you minimize a known risk to better manage your way out of or around a potential failure?

Not surprisingly, our second business crisis had amazing similarities to our first. After The Company Store, we had established a new beachhead in the business-to-business category, and the primary account in the category was a company called New England Business Service, or NEBS. The mini-crisis was precipitated once again by NEBS becoming our new mini-gorilla.

At this point, you might ask, "Geez, didn't you guys learn your lesson the first time?" The correct Jeopardy answer is, "What is 'Yes, but we couldn't say no?'" (See the "never give another agency your scraps" reference earlier in this chapter.)

Here's how it happened: When an agency connects with a client, it is magic. The client grows wildly and the agency must grow wildly in turn to keep up with the demand. The agency creates a marketing vehicle that delivers for the client. The client is excited and asks the agency to create five more just like it. Before you know it, you are eyeball-to-eyeball with explosive growth and there is no way to shut it off unless you refuse the business, which I have never been able to do.

We had moved from the glamour of down-filled coats and luxurious bedroom furnishings to a company whose main business was selling checks to small businesses. Why the big change? I think having worked in a niche category for many years and being given the "opportunity" to discover new areas (an opportunity such as when a client fires you and you need a new client!), we overreacted and explored areas that were about as far from where our interests were once rooted as we could get—simply for a change of scenery. (Kind of like the palpable night-and-day difference in demeanor between my first wife and my second wife. I love them both, but they are decidedly different.) NEBS became as great a client for us as The Company Store had once been. At the time we worked with NEBS, it was a billion-dollar company. (Note: NEBS was purchased in 2004, two years after we stopped working for them, by Deluxe Corporation, a competitor whose main business is also checks, much the same way The Company Store was sold to their competitor. There are a lot of patterns in business!) NEBS had a database of nearly a million buyers of essentially a single product: checks. And similar to most businesses, they wanted to diversify into new areas, where they unfortunately had no experience, but the main idea for many companies with large databases is to utilize that valuable asset to sell things other than paper checks. NEBS was fearful of being reliant on checks because the digital age had arrived and they feared checks would go the way Kodak film eventually did. It is further evidence that we live in a fast-changing world when even the big boys and girls have to pay close attention to the markets around them. We are all only one or two steps away from total extinction when new product innovations can make old product categories such as film and checks obsolete overnight.

We helped NEBS with many of its entrepreneurial marketing efforts that would have been difficult for them within the confines of their disciplined, single-focus, billion-dollar culture. Ovation was the perfect conduit for entrepreneurial experimentation into new markets. We helped them market logoed merchandise to business owners that were loyal buyers of their checks. The customers made the mental leap that if this company could deliver quality paper checks with a business logo on it, it could also deliver a sports shirt with that same logo on the pocket. NEBS had almost a million loyal buyers who would soon be buying work shirts, hats, jackets, and sports shirts with business logos affixed to the merchandise.

Sadly, the average length of agency-client relationships has now fallen to just under three years. We worked with NEBS for nearly 10, but the end was, of course, inevitable. NEBS appointed a new president and in his opening remarks to the company he was quoted as saying he enjoys working with suppliers in his backyard. NEBS was located in Groton, Massachusetts; we were located in La Crosse, Wisconsin—a distance of 991 miles. It was the beginning of the end. Being the wily veterans we had become at handling such events, we had again neutralized the gorilla, so when the end finally came we took the loss in stride.

When a company does experience really bad news, the kind that threatens your core existence, or the lifestyle to which you have grown accustomed to living, and everything around the leader starts going to hell, it is the leader's responsibility to remain cool under fire, to keep everyone focused on defining and then solving the problem, and to convince the company that we can get through this trauma (the mere act of believing that you can do it is 90 percent of succeeding). Like it or not, the leader must become the "we can do it" guy, because other people in the organization will be overly focused on possible negative outcomes. Worst-case, some people will be panicked and scared, two traits you need least in a crisis. Generally, the further down from the top you go in an organization the more fearful people will become because they have the least control in resolving the crisis. Communicating up and down the organization is key. Weekly fireside chats are essential to bring control and confidence to the company. Employees will be far more comfortable if you tell them what you are doing to lead them out of the crisis.

Negativity is a sad affliction of today's celebrity-driven society, as it is far more hip and safe to appear negative. Weak leaders fear positioning themselves too optimistically about the chances of overcoming a crisis and returning to good times, because if you are overly positive and things go from bad to worse, weak leaders feel they will appear poorly in the eyes of their coworkers. (The idea being, not only did he help run the ship into the ground, but he also had the nerve to think he could correct the problem and make things right again.) But if leaders are overly negative from the beginning and things turn from bad to good, and the company starts celebrating, no one will care that one of the leaders was so negative because the ship has been righted, all is well, and everyone is celebrating and will forgive anyone who was negative during the crisis because, after all, there was good reason to be pessimistic.

The problem with playing it safe, covering your ass, and laying low in a crisis is that this is the very moment when leaders must inspire. Your chances of winning magnify many times over if strong leaders stick their necks out a mile and come forward to inspire the troops by proclaiming, "We can do this and here is 'the plan' that details how we are going to win!"

During a time of crisis, the quote that I consistently turn to for inspiration and direction is the one at the beginning of this chapter from William Shakespeare: "Cowards die many times before their deaths. The valiant never taste of death but once." The quote instills in me freedom from fear; the absence of fear is critical to winning. You must remain creative and in a heightened state of superior problem-solving ability to work your way out of difficult situations. You can't do that if you are gripped by fear. Some presence of fear is a positive motivator and awakens our senses, but too much and you stand a chance to lose the essential "can-do" swagger that draws people to a leader. The quote says to me that I am allowed fear one time, just before I meet death, but until that time I will fearlessly confront and subsequently solve my company's problems. A bit dramatic perhaps, but it has worked each time I have managed my way successfully through a crisis.

CHAPTER INSIGHTS
Shit Happens

- **Face your gorilla.** What is the monster that keeps you up nights? Confronting it by formulating a reasoned plan of attack, before a crisis situation, will allow you to neutralize or tame the gorilla and get on with business.

- **Develop your worst-case scenario.** What could the gorilla do to disrupt your business? For each foreseeable event strategize a first step to protect your interests.

- **What can you do right now?** Of the strategies and plans you've come up with, what reasonable actions can you take now, before a crisis happens?

26

Blow It Up

Some people think it's holding on that makes one
strong; sometimes it's letting go.
—Sylvia Robinson

In Chapter 8, and throughout this book, we have discussed the theory of "continuous improvement." It is logical to make slow and steady improvements to everything we do. Most of us invest well-intentioned, mostly productive time tweaking existing systems, products, ad campaigns, ideas, and so on, to make them perform better. Continuous improvement is the gold standard by which successful people and ideas move to ever-greater heights, and the theory most often produces outstanding results. However, occasionally the system you are trying to improve is flawed beyond fixing. Sometimes the system needs to be "blown up."

An example of blowing up and starting over happened at our agency when we were changing the way we handled our (seemingly simple) procedure of paging an associate for a client phone call. We had always prided ourselves on quick and responsive service. So when a client called and an associate was not in his or her office, as associates rarely were, we paged them over our intercom system for everyone to hear. The paging became a way of life and grew beyond its original scope. We paged to announce the start of staff meetings ("The Microsoft creative review is starting in the main conference room."); we paged for package deliveries; we paged for, well, just about any situation.

As our paging frequency grew, the sound of continual announcements blaring over the intercom made the office sound like a Greyhound bus station! None of us were happy with the constant interruptions. Several attempts were made at "continuous improvements" to fix the problem, but, alas, nothing worked. So after years of aggravation, interruptions, and failed temporary attempts at improving the paging system, we decided to blow it up.

One day we simply announced that we would page no more. Interestingly, we did not offer any alternatives to establish a new system. We let the system work to establish its own new flow of information, which is the most natural way to allow systems to self-correct. It's like pouring water downhill; the water does an outstanding job of establishing its own natural path to the ocean. Not surprisingly, with paging no longer an option, people became more creative in solving the problem.

There were some initially rocky steps to eliminating paging. Our friendly receptionist wanted to kill me. Losing the convenience of paging momentarily frustrated people who needed to find another associate to move forward on a project. However, most of us quickly came to appreciate the quiet and were grateful that the annoying noise and interruptions of our paging system were gone for good. Eventually, our resourceful associates started to find new and better ways to locate their fellow associates without paging. For example, without paging to start a meeting, everyone just figured out they needed to be there when the meeting was scheduled to start. (What a concept!)

We eventually came up with a simple idea for those associates who received the most phone calls to keep the front

> ## The Failure Factor
> Know when to start fresh. Not everything can be, or should be, fixed. Persistent "patching" of a failing project can temporarily support inefficiency and make success impossible. Sometimes a fresh start is what it takes to succeed.

desk informed of their whereabouts. Then, if a client called, the receptionist knew immediately what to say to the client, and could either find the person or tell the client when to expect a return call. In the past, paging had taken up to 30 seconds to search for the associates. If they were in a meeting, they simply could not hear and did not respond to the page, which sent us back to the phone to say something ridiculous like, "I can't find Jane right now; can I have her call you?" (when I'm able to locate her). The new way made us sound a lot smarter to clients needing to talk to our people. Eventually, the technology of a new central telephone system and the dreaded prerecorded voice answering the phone for corporate America led to a whole new set of challenges.

If you have not made the progress you hoped for with small, continuous improvements, be bold and blow it up. The experience can be exhilarating, and the results will probably surprise you, as they did us. Not only did we survive the experience, but our people and our business also grew more confident and creative in solving problems.

CHAPTER INSIGHTS
What Do You Need to Begin Again?

- **What problem or obstacle have you been tinkering with for too long?** Are you wasting more energy trying to fix it than it is worth? Sometimes we try to fix things that have outlived their usefulness. The problems we experience with them can be a sign that they no longer serve a purpose in our lives. If they are truly necessary, perhaps they are beyond patching. Perhaps it is time to blow it up.

- **Do you perceive starting over as a failure?** Accepting endings and moving on to new solutions gives purpose to learning from experience. Based on what you've learned, you are now able to make the leap to the next level.

27
Why Wait?

*Things may come to those who wait...but only the
things left by those who hustle.*
—Abraham Lincoln

The word is *wait*. I think this word is one of the ugliest
words in the English language. *Wait* is a word used by
those who fear progress and forward motion. *Wait* is a word
used by those who fear change. *Wait* is a word used by those
who fear failure. The word *wait* drains energy and the enthusiasm for ideas.

I cannot understand why anyone, particularly a leader,
would utter the word *wait* under the pretense of directing
his or her team toward a desired action.

A common use of the word *wait* is for the leader to say,
"We want to wait before we move forward." Even though we
have this hot new idea, we want to wait. I always wonder:
wait for what? Wait for a world-class risk-taker to come in
and take your prize by advancing with his or her idea?

Wait is often used in advertising agencies as a call for
inaction. People will say, "I can't go forward with that. I don't
have enough information, so I will have to wait until I get
more information."

Wait is used by people to procrastinate. It takes nerve
and guts to move forward with ideas, and, if you fall back on
the word *wait*, you are suddenly relieved of your responsibility to move forward in life because now it's okay to wait.

As you wait you carry a weight, the burden of inaction. I
think it's an interesting coincidence that these homonyms

share the meaning of carrying a burden. If we listen deeply, words can sometimes say more than we initially hear.

I should clarify that waiting because of fear is different from waiting for a strategic opening or the ideal timing. It is important to fully appreciate the differences. And, I must confess, at times, I struggle with the concept of waiting. Let me give you an example:

I spend most weekends during the summer racing my bicycle. Because of my disdain for waiting, I am a mediocre bike racer. Bike racing is different from most sports in that the bike racer who goes to the front of the pack and stays at the front expends the most energy cutting through the wind and generally loses the race. On the other hand, the racer who sits in the pack and drafts off of the other cyclists in front of him most often has the most energy left at the end to win the sprint. My coach has tried to counsel me in this technique. He has sent me eloquent reminders that the winners of the bike race are not the leaders who charge boldly to the front and stay out front. I seldom win bike races, because I do not have the patience to wait. What has made me weak in bike racing has made me strong in business. The two sports are worlds apart.

> ### The Failure Factor
> Take action. Move forward along the path, even if your first attempt ends in failure, as ultimately you will achieve success. Sometimes you take a giant leap ahead and sometimes you take a tiny step. You'll get there.

In the advertising business, those who have ideas, either new product ideas or new advertising ideas, and those who hit the marketplace first with them, are the ones who win. In every product and service category, with few exceptions, the first successful product to enter the market and the consumer's mind easily holds its market share and retains its number-one position. So when someone has a hot idea for a new product, the last thing you want to do is wait.

For some people, I think waiting becomes a way to avoid their fear of failure. If you wait, you take no risks, you make no statements, and you try nothing new. Waiting is complete inactivity. Failure is delayed—yet so is success. Those who wait are more motivated to avoid the pain of failure than to experience the joy of success.

The opposite of waiting is to take action, to move forward with your thoughts and ideas to accomplish something, instead of waiting for something—or nothing—to happen. I am in agreement with the words of Johann Wolfgang von Goethe: "Whatever you can do, or dream you can, begin it. Boldness has genius, power, and magic in it."

CHAPTER INSIGHTS
Move Forward

- **What are your obstacles? What are your fears?** You may see physical obstacles, such as money, or mental obstacles, such as knowledge. If fear of failure is holding you back, develop a worst-case scenario plan to examine your fears. What are you risking by trying? What will you learn by trying? What will you lose by *not* trying?
- **Establish your goals.** Set them high. Include push goals that you are likely to fail at the first time you try.
- **Write down your goals.** Break each goal down into actions that can be more easily accomplished. Make notes of your actions and outcomes, whether you succeeded or failed, and the lesson you learned as a result.
- **Begin.**

28

I Can't Find My Ball

Success seems to be connected to action.
Successful people keep moving. They make
mistakes, but they don't quit.
—Conrad Hilton

When I was a little kid my dad and I used to play golf. Children often hit the ball in the wrong direction and lose it, and those with short attention spans forget where we hit the ball just as soon as we walk to find it. I was set up to fail at golf because you receive a one-stroke penalty if you lose your ball (plus, it's expensive).

So after a few frustrating "moments" searching in vain for my lost ball, I would stop dead in my tracks and yell, "I can't find my ball." Patience is another one of those attributes you need in golf. My dad used this father-and-son Kodak moment to teach, saying, "You will never find your golf ball standing in one place." That struck me as profound even at age 7. He went on to explain that you've got to cover a lot of territory, moving quickly in many different directions, to find a lost golf ball. I saved a lot of money throughout the years because I listened to my dad and most often found my ball. And I am certain the philosophy helped me in business.

Business has a lot of moments when you do the equivalent of losing your golf ball. You can stand in the same place screaming, "I can't find my ball," or you can keep moving and trying new tactics and strategies to turn things around. If demand for your product is dwindling, you've got to find a new audience or new way to package your current offering—a new version, perhaps, or move on to an entirely new product.

You can't stand in the same place trying the same thing because if it isn't working, if there is no demand, chances are slim that the situation is going to change anytime soon, much like standing in one place looking for a golf ball that isn't there.

Think of the product changes that occurred in just the last few years. We went from floppy disks to zip drives to memory sticks in the blink of an eye. So as the leader of Acme Floppy Disks you could be passing out huge Christmas bonuses one year and layoff notices the next. Was Acme Floppy Disk moving in different directions trying to reinvent itself, or was it standing in one place screaming about not being able to find new product sales?

More than 10 years ago, Kodak meant film, and its stock price soared above $90 per share. Today, Kodak is adapting to the digital world by selling cameras, memory sticks, digital picture frames, and other related merchandise. Kodak's stock price is now around $4 or $5 dollars per share. You can find film on their Website, but it is no longer driving the proverbial train. Plus, while they were coming to grips with the reality of the world going digital, Fuji stepped in, ate Kodak's lunch, and helped themselves to a huge share of what little film business was left. Some days it doesn't pay to get out of bed.

Kodak had the resources to keep searching for their golf ball and allocated money for product research and development to be competitive in the new digital world. But did they embrace the possibility of failure immediately? Prominent business writers have written that Kodak was in denial about the digital revolution and moved far too slowly to embrace the change necessary to replace their biggest source of income. I liken it to the business world's reluctance to embrace even the possibility of failure. Kodak had been making its living for decades from film. And it is extremely difficult for executives, who are making $200,000 to $2 million a year, to transport themselves a few years into the future and visualize their world crumbling. If failure weren't such a big bad boogieman, such a giant mental hurdle to climb, they could have seen it coming and had far more time to plan for the inevitable. But it is so easy to be in denial when you are making buckets of money.

So what chance do those of us managing small companies with limited resources have as our businesses' chal-

> **The Failure Factor**
>
> Keep moving. Keep your eyes open. Keep asking questions. If you stand still, the only people who will succeed are your competitors, because you make an excellent target.

lenges continue to change and evolve and the potential for failure comes knocking? If we embrace the possibility of failure as a way to learn, look boldly into the future, and keep moving our businesses rapidly in different directions, testing new ways to survive, we will improve our chances of staying alive with the change that surrounds us.

To support failure as a tool, job one is to let your associates know that they are empowered to try new things that will not always work, and that is okay. They will be rewarded richly if they succeed, and they will be allowed to survive if they fail. The smartest of companies will publicly reward failure and those with the "cajones" to step up and make the attempt to try something new, bold, and daring. You are up against decades of ingrained learning that taught us to stay below the radar, take no risks, make no waves, and, whatever you do, don't fail. Leaders must instill that adventurous, entrepreneurial spirit back into the workforce.

Employee-owned control is an important first step toward gaining the ability to see future business challenges. Employees make their best decisions when they are fearless and have control over their own destiny. And there is a good chance you will kill them if you don't let them control their own lives. A new Japanese study (yet another study with the same basic findings) published in *Men's Health* (April 2009) found that "...men with demanding jobs in which they feel micromanaged have a 2 1/2 times higher risk of stroke than men in less taxing positions."

In addition to killing your best people, micromanagement also kills creativity and innovation. If you've been told what you can and can't put up in your own office cubicle, how are you ever going to see the digital revolution coming at you like a bullet train? You won't see it because you've been told by the culture of your company not to think for yourself. Micromanaged people instinctively learn to play it safe and stay below the radar. To find the next great trend in business, you can't be fearful of your actions. You've got to take bold steps into the unknown and try new stuff. And if you fail, try more new stuff until something great happens—and great things *will* happen if you stay at it long enough and remain fearless.

To further complicate leadership, there is a certain type of worker that actually seeks protection and prefers to be controlled; after all, it is safe to be told what to do. You make no decisions and take no risks when you are told not to put a picture up in your cubicle. If you are given control and told that you can now display pictures that are "deemed appropriate," you must now make a cultural decision.

When I managed an ad agency, I was continually asked to approve purchase orders for everything from travel to computers to books—the normal stuff. It occurred to me that it was easy for people to hand me a purchase order and ask if it was okay if they bought it. They took no risks and had nothing invested in the decision. It became my decision, and when the purchase is a substantial investment or "major initiative" it *should* be the leader's decision. But if you wanted to spend $1,000 of the company's money to attend a conference, what risk do you take if I make the spending decision? So I announced that my approval would no longer be required on minor purchases. It was up to the individuals to decide for themselves if this would be a wise investment in company spending.

I made the announcement and explained the policy, and guess what I kept receiving? Yes, purchase orders. About half of my associates were extremely uncomfortable making their own spending decision. So I pulled some of them aside and said, "Didn't you understand the new policy? You approve your own expenditures."

In reply, I would hear something like, "Well, yes, but I thought this was important and so I wanted you to take a look at it." What they wanted me to do was take the decision process back out of their hands. They didn't want to have to think about the responsibility of spending company money in such a way, perhaps in part because no one ever gave them such control.

So I called yet another company meeting. I presoaked some of the purchase orders in lighter fluid and it made a rather dramatic presentation when I lit the papers on fire and said I wanted them to make future spending decisions. Throughout the next year, travel expenses dropped 70 percent, mileage expenses dropped 46 percent, entertainment spending was down 39 percent, and office supplies were reduced by 18 percent, while business increased 16 percent. They clearly gave the spending decision more thought because it became their responsibility and not mine.

So if you can't find your golf ball or your business direction, start moving quickly in different directions and try new stuff. Mentally attack and reinvent yourself every day and embrace failure as your friend to improved learning. Sometimes it even helps to pretend you are a bit neurotic and the world is out to get you. Because, guess what? The world is out to get you! Someone is always trying to stick their hand in your pocket and take your hard-earned money or steal your ideas. They'd even steal your golf ball if you gave them half a chance.

CHAPTER INSIGHTS
Eyes Wide Open, Questioning What You See

- **Think like an inventor.** Inventors and change masters aren't all geniuses, but they know one thing the rest of us don't: how to ask the simple, sometimes childlike questions that no one else bothers to ask. What if bread was rectangular instead of round? How could a parking ramp be more space efficient? How could we make a tire that never goes flat?

- **Take a swing.** Prototyping is one of the primary tools of inventors and innovators. Consider your company's product or an item you use every day. If you could remake it, how many options are possible? Sometimes it helps to imagine cost is no option, but other times, reducing cost actually leads to the breakthrough idea. For example: How could it be less expensive? Refillable package design or self-serve purchase. How could it operate on an alternative energy source? Crank flashlight, solar hot water heater, or wind turbine. Smaller? Pocket fishing rod or laptop computer. Safer? Hands-free phone earpiece or motion-sensitive entry. Could it be combined with another product? Camera phone or TV/computer.

- **Where's your ball?** If you think change won't totally transform your product or your business, think about how many everyday items or services you wouldn't want to live without, that didn't exist five, 10, 25, or 50 years ago. Wireless Internet? Online banking? Your portable computer? TiVo? Microwave ovens? Mobile phone/camera/Web? Now that your eye is on the ball, take a swing.

29

It's the Economy, Stupid

Success is not fatal, failure is not final: it is the courage to continue that counts.
—Winston Churchill

I supported President Obama's candidacy with my time and my money. It is hard to keep that kind of thing a secret these days. If you Google "Ralph Heath" you can easily find out how much I donated to the campaign. I understand the public's need to know who supports our candidates, but I've always had a romantic vision of the secret ballot. Now when you donate to a candidate it is out there for the world to see. Thus far, I'm only mildly uncomfortable with Obama's presidency. However, I cringed the other day when he said we weren't going to "look back" while attempting to solve the current economic crisis (February 2009).

I guess we all know what he meant in general "rah-rah" terms, but not looking back to celebrate and learn from our failures is one of our biggest problems in the process of "fixing" past mistakes. It is why I advocate celebrating failure—using our past mistakes as a method to learn from our experience and not repeat our mistakes in the future. When you begin the process of looking back to study why the system broke down, it appears to people that you will quickly be finger-pointing and placing blame. That is immediately perceived as a bad thing because we *loathe* mistakes and failures rather then *celebrate* them as learning opportunities. Next, the people being blamed will make excuses for their mistakes and claim that it wasn't their fault and become extremely defensive about their part in the problem. What we need for them to say instead is, "Yes, I was out there on the front lines trying my best and I failed. I've analyzed what I did wrong and here is the solution to the problem that will ensure it never happens again."

But they'll make up wild stories explaining how they had nothing to do with it and they'll start finger-pointing at others. Almost simultaneously, another group will jump into high gear blaming those who are close to the scene of the crime for their part in the financial collapse of the world and they'll start calling for heads to roll. After all, someone must be held accountable and punished for all the misery and losses that our country, our people, and others around the world are suffering.

That is what we do to people who screw up: We fire the sons-of-bitches in a very public way because they are perceived as bad people. We learn nothing when we follow this path, but it somehow makes us feel better that *some* kind of action was taken, even if it was the wrong action. But what if many of these people aren't bad people? What if they are just like you and me and they were trying to do their best to keep a global economy firing on all cylinders? After all, how easy can it be to lead a complex global economy?

The problem with not looking back and analyzing our country's failures is that it will solve nothing, and, worse yet, we will learn nothing and will be certain to repeat our failures. What if we treated "failure" in a whole different light? Did either presidential candidate John McCain's

> ## The Failure Factor
>
> Take responsibility. If you acknowledge the mistake, failure, or problem, but blame someone else, it just makes you look powerless (and a little stupid) for doing nothing but pointing your finger. We're in this together. When did we give up being Americans to be merely a Democrat or a Republican?

economic advisor, former Senator Phil Gramm (R), or Congressman Barney Frank (D) want to see the world's economic system collapse when Gramm advocated deregulation and Frank advocated making loans easier to obtain for people with less wealth? I am certain they were both simply doing what they thought was best for the country (and maybe a little bit for their own political future).

Did the past presidents of Citibank build one of the largest banks in the world so that, if the bank became big enough, the government couldn't possibly let their business collapse if the worst happened? I don't think so. I think they were doing their jobs, buying up other banks, and merging with other financial institutions because they thought it would make more money for their shareholders and they would be viewed as heroes, rather than the villains they are perceived as today. I'm not saying there aren't any bad guys in this economic soap opera, because there are, but I am saying there were a lot of good people who tried to do their best, and guess what? They failed. That is what often happens when you are trying your best. If we created a culture in which we could rationally discuss our failures and analyze where we went wrong without trying to lynch the people who made the mistakes, we would learn more from our past failures, avoid repeating the mistakes, and save ourselves from the accompanying misery.

Lance Armstrong is a believer in analyzing failure to achieve success (read his quote at the beginning of Chapter 12). He may be attempting to win the Tour de France for the eighth time in the summer of 2009. Imagine that he fails in that attempt. Should he then fire his coach, who has been with him for all previous seven victories, without "looking back" and analyzing where his training perhaps took a wrong turn? Or should he sit down with his coach, who has been in the trenches with him through many ups and downs and review his prerace preparation? Which coach would you most want writing the plan and leading the charge to win the Tour de France the following year? I'd want the guy who learned what he did wrong and probably now knows how to fix it after he suffered through a failure. That failed coach now has the best possible preparation as he has experienced both success and failure, and is therefore loaded with as much insightful information as possible. I'd pick the guy who failed at number eight before I'd go on the market for a new coach who has no experience base with the athlete's unique "engine" and his latest possible collapse (if he indeed collapses). In fact, Armstrong's coach would be a far smarter coach going for win number nine than he was when they went for win number eight because of the knowledge that failure can bring to the process, if you embrace it. That is the whole premise of *Celebrating Failure*.

I know some will say they hate to dwell on failure for fear it is some kind of contagious disease. But it is clearly not contagious if you have the wisdom to embrace it as a badge of honor and a learning tool.

One of the publishers who initially reviewed the manuscript for this book said my book didn't pass "the subway test." (If you're like me you've probably never heard of the subway test. The subway test supposedly says that no one wants to be seen on the subway reading a book about failure.) I nearly screamed out loud when I heard that and immediately signed with Career Press, who had the cajones to embrace a book with *failure* in the title. Therein lies the problem with most businesses that do not use failure as a tool to achieve success. Their fear of failure is so powerful they cannot think about failure, they cannot be associated with failure (even on a book cover), and they cannot examine their failures to understand what went wrong.

> *Those who fail to learn from history are condemned to repeat it.*
> —Winston Churchill

CHAPTER INSIGHTS
History 101

Not being a history professor, I cannot presume to teach it to others. However, what I do know for certain about history is from my personal experience, and experience is the best teacher. The lessons I have learned from my experience with my mistakes and failures are the greatest lessons life has given me. To me, *Celebrating Failure* is how I strive to learn my lessons well—so as not to repeat them again.

For inspiration in facing failures and analyzing my personal history and the lessons it teaches, I often turn to the words of other writers, poets, and leaders—people who express their thoughts more gracefully than I. Here are some of their words.

History, despite its wrenching pain, cannot be unlived, but if faced with courage, need not be lived again.
—Maya Angelou

History is a guide to navigate in perilous times. History is who we are and why we are the way we are.
—David C. McCullough

History has demonstrated that the most notable winners usually encountered heartbreaking obstacles before they triumphed. They won because they refused to become discouraged by their defeats.
—B.C. Forbes (founder of *Forbes* magazine)

30

Change Is My Drug of Choice

I've missed more than 9,000 shots in my career.
I've lost almost 300 games. 26 times, I've been
trusted to take the game-winning shot and
missed. I've failed over and over and over again
in my life. And that is why I succeed.
—Michael Jordan

I was involved in a unique business experience with Ovation Marketing that few people on this planet will ever experience. I was able to start an advertising agency with no money and, with the help of an incredibly loyal group of people, build it into a company that averaged $25 million a year in capitalized billings, and employed an average of 30-plus associates. And then, after 31 years, we decided to close it and move on to new adventures and new life experiences.

I love change. I thrive on it. It makes me high. Change is my drug of choice. It doesn't matter to me if it is a business change or a bike course I've never been on—the senses awaken when you are exposed to new adventures.

My best case for change occurred with my first "real" job. Right out of college, I managed a radio station for six years. As part of my radio work, I would write (my first love) commercials and people would say, "We like your radio ads; how would you like to do our television and print ads as well?" And thus was born Ovation Marketing. I loved the radio station job and the steady paycheck, but the lure to change and play with new media was too great, so I quit the radio job and made at least $13,000 that first year working for myself. I thought this was great—not the initial money, but the changing jobs. You do something for five or six years and then you change jobs and find something new; that was exciting to me.

Now, 31 years later, I wonder how I ended up flirting with the longevity record for ad-agency ownership. I think it says a lot about the people I worked with. I was simply having too much fun to change jobs. It was hard to get off of the stage. Several times, when things got difficult, as they always do (especially with ad agencies), I thought about leaving, but then I thought, *I can't leave when times are tough. I will wait and help turn it around.* And as soon as things turned around, I was having too much fun again to leave.

Ideally, an entrepreneur (and I am one) wants to build a company that continues on into the future without him. Ovation failed to pass that hurdle, but by most all other measurements, especially financially (the main way we keep score), it was extremely successful. Throughout the years I had probably 25 serious opportunities to sell the business. None of them ever interested me because I was always having too much fun to sell, and because it made some of my loyal associates nervous—especially my outstanding middle-management team, as they assumed, wrongly I believed, that their jobs would be lost in some cost-cutting move. I also didn't want to sell because I knew I wouldn't last two days working for someone else (and I might be exaggerating about the second day), and finally because selling an ad agency is extremely difficult under the best of circumstances.

No one will pay cash in advance for an agency. They will pay you out of the cash flow your business generates throughout a period of five to 10 years. So you build up relationships with clients, and then you announce you are leaving and you try and sell those relationships and the business you are conducting to strangers. Yet you don't really own the relationships. You have simply brought together a group of talented people to manage the relationships and do great creative work. Selling an agency to outsiders is tenuous at best.

What I really wanted to do at some point in time (and that point in time never came) was to sell the remaining 60 percent of Ovation to my associates. I somewhat naïvely thought it wouldn't be that big of a deal to find a new leader, pass the baton, step aside, and move on to other challenges, and maybe under the right circumstances it wouldn't have been. But we soon faced the perfect storm.

Eager for change, I had been testing other career opportunities, and in 2007 I reached out to an aspiring serious presidential candidate whom I greatly admired. (I am honoring a promise I made not to write about the experience—not an easy promise for a writer—other than to say it was an extremely positive and rewarding learning experience.) My stated goal and purpose was to help him get elected president of the United States. I know it sounds odd just to write those words, but that is what the entrepreneurial side of me wanted to do with my life in 2007. Much to my surprise, the candidate accepted my invitation to help. I thought it would be a great way to transition out of the agency business and into a relatively new career in which I could use my management and marketing skills, especially with the communications and fundraising potential of the Internet (which Obama used to near perfection). The candidate, whom I admire greatly, made it clear from the start that he had not yet decided to seek the highest office in the land, although he was considering a run and was mentioned prominently in national polls. Let me make it clear that we are talking a long shot here, similar to the guy who eventually ended up winning the job. I worked for said candidate for about a year until he eventually decided, to my disappointment, that he did not wish to seek the presidency in 2008. I exited on the best of terms immediately after his official announcement to the press, and greatly admire that organization and the confidence they had to allow me to become involved in their group. They work in a different and exciting world.

Undeterred in seeking new entrepreneurial career opportunities, I decided to finish the book I had been working on for 20 years—the book you hold in your hand—and find an agent and publisher in the summer of 2008.

I confess I haven't found career changes difficult, scary, or stressful. In less then two years, I had joined with an extremely well respected literary agent, a major book publisher, and a top contender for the presidency of the United States. Change is good, and each time I have climbed out of the nest, I have had the time of my life.

So to initially begin my idea to sell the agency to my associates, I asked one of my talented and competent vice presidents at Ovation to step into my job while I gracefully left the stage for my first loves: a writing and speaking career. And this is the part where things start to get complicated. Ovation's two largest clients, Anheuser-Busch and Aearo Technologies, were almost simultaneously acquired by large multinational corporations, InBev and 3M, respectively. The relationships we had built throughout the years within those organizations and their reasons for hiring us changed quickly. The new corporate marketing teams had new ways of doing business and different priorities. On top of that, the national economy was going rapidly downhill and marketing initiatives at Fortune 500 companies, the lifeblood of Ovation Marketing throughout its 31-year history, were placed on hold. In the fall and winter of 2008/2009, no one was looking to start a new one-to-one marketing initiative to connect with his or her customers, and that is what Ovation did best.

Although we could have continued with the agency business, building Ovation's business back up with clients of the caliber of Anheuser-Busch and Aearo Technologies would have taken tremendous time, energy, and money at a time when I was trying to exit the business and publish and market my book. In consultation with my agency partners, we decided to simply close Ovation Marketing and move on to new adventures. Although you would like to propel your startup of 31 years ago into the future, you develop other priorities, and the time to celebrate a success and move on was right.

Would I do anything differently? Not really. From a strictly financial standpoint, some might say I should have more actively pursued the offers to purchase Ovation and attempted to cash out years ago and perhaps make more money than I did holding on to the company as long as I have, but even that is questionable at best; the stars and the moon have to be in near perfect alignment to "cash out" from an ad agency. Plus, I never wanted to sell.

Was Ovation similar to many ad agencies that end up being too reliant on too few large accounts? Absolutely, almost since day one; as with most other successful agencies, it goes with the territory. I wrote in an earlier chapter about an agency's need to constantly neutralize the gorilla client. It is a problem we were aware of, and we were always trying to diversify our client base.

At some point in time it is best to say "enough." That was fun. Pretty much 31 years of fun. I had the time of my life and have nothing else to prove in the ad agency arena. Now I'd like to try something new and different, because change is good.

I know now that I am a serial entrepreneur. When an entrepreneur starts a business and it grows into an entity that needs discipline, processes, and long-term strategic planning, the entrepreneur must either leave and start another new company, or see if he has the ability to successfully manage what he started, which takes an entirely different skill set from starting a company. I am comfortable in the knowledge that I can do both. If you held a gun to my head and said, "You must choose between a lifetime of entrepreneur start-ups or long-term management or we'll shoot you," I would say, "Shoot me." I love them both. Change is good.

CHAPTER INSIGHTS
Closing a Door—Opening a Window

- **Change and failure.** Do you ever find yourself mistaking change for failure? Change is transformation. Failure is the lack of success. Change is certain. Failure is not. Are you avoiding change in your life because you fear you could fail?

- **Let go of your fear.** Did you know they have a word for fear of failure? Atychiphobia. The definition is an extreme, irrational fear that keeps you from doing something you want to do. That's no way to go through life. Some people are afraid of the unknown future that change represents. Some people are even afraid of success because if they cannot sustain their success they will consider themselves a failure!

  Don't let fear limit your life. Take action. Whatever you're afraid of doing, do it. Take a small step or take a huge leap. As an advertising man, an athlete, and a business coach, my advice to overcome fear is to follow Nike's famous tagline and "just do it."

  Get out there and start doing, making mistakes, and failing. Then celebrate your failures, because every time you fail you learn more about how to succeed.

Postmortem

I need your help. One of the basic premises of this book is to encourage you, the reader, to analyze whatever you do in life to continuously improve. I would love to hear from you on how you would improve *Celebrating Failure*.

I have started a second book tentatively titled *Thoughtful Leadership*. Your comments and insights would be extremely important to me as I continue to write. As discussed throughout *Celebrating Failure*, the best chance for improvement lies most often in our failures, but I am interested in hearing all of your comments and suggestions, and would be eternally grateful for your insights. (Have you ever noticed the great restaurants always ask about the service and food? The bad ones never ask. I'm trying to be like a great restaurant.)

I will try my best to respond personally to your comments and use your advice and direction to improve my future efforts. Thank you in advance for your help.

Contact me through my Thoughtful Leadership and Marketing blog, *www.RalphHeath.com*; at my book's Website, *www.CelebratingFailure.com*; or by phone at (608) 785-1500.

You can write to me at:
Ralph Heath
Heath Leadership Group
201 Main Street
Suite 902
La Crosse, WI 54601

Index

About the Author

Ralph Heath is an author, business coach, consultant, and motivational speaker. He is president of the Heath Leadership Group, a firm specializing in helping individuals and businesses achieve their full potential. Heath calls upon his 30-plus years of wildly diverse business experience to help clients solve their unique challenges. Ralph Heath's blog, Thoughtful Leadership and Marketing, can be found at *www.ralphheath.com*.

Heath was previously president of Ovation Marketing, an ad agency he founded in 1978 in La Crosse, Wisconsin. Ovation was twice named to *Inc.* magazine's 500 fastest-growing companies. While at Ovation, Heath's work was recognized with a John Caples International Advertising Award and he was named Midwest Direct Marketer of the Year.

He earned his BS in mass communications from the University of Wisconsin–La Crosse. His experience includes motivational speaking and teaching advertising/marketing courses at the University of Wisconsin.

He is active in the La Crosse community, serving as past president of two nonprofit organizations, the Mississippi Valley Conservancy and Human Powered Trails. Heath is a passionate advocate of exercise and a healthy lifestyle. He is a founding member of the La Crosse Fitness Festival (*www.lacrossefitnessfestival.com*), has been honored as a four-time Triathlon All-American, is a two-time finisher of the Hawaii Ironman, and is a bronze medalist in Wisconsin cycling (2008).